REMINISCENCES

1827 - 1897

GOVERNOR ROBERT M. McLANE

SR *Scholarly Resources Inc.*
Wilmington, Delaware

SCHOLARLY RESOURCES, INC.
1508 Pennsylvania Avenue
Wilmington, Delaware 19806

Reprint edition published in 1972
First edition privately printed in 1903

Library of Congress Catalog Card Number: 72-79831
ISBN: 0-8420-1375-x

Manufactured in the United States of America

GOVERNOR ROBERT M. M^CLANE'S

REMINISCENCES

—

1827 - 1889

—

I VISITED my father in Washington during the winter of 1827-28, when the final coalition was effected between the original friends of General Jackson who had supported him for the Presidency in 1824, and the friends of Mr. Crawford, who was the Caucus nominee of the Democratic Party in that year. My father, who was a Senator from Delaware, was living on Seventh-street, at a well-known Congressional Mess, the members of which were among the most influential friends of Mr. Crawford. I remember Messrs. Van Buren and Cambreling of New York, Mr. Forsyth of Georgia, Colonel Drayton of South Carolina, and

Mr. Archer of Virginia. I remember, in the same intimate association at this time Messrs. MacDuffie, Hayne, and Hamilton of South Carolina, Cuthbert of Georgia, Stevenson and Rives of Virginia, Buchanan of Pennsylvania, White and Eaton of Tennessee, King of Alabama, and Livingston of Louisiana.

Among the friends of Mr. Crawford, none exerted greater influence or commanded more respect than my father and Mr. Van Buren. They had been his special friends during the Monroe Administration and pending the Presidential Election of 1824. Mr. Crawford's health had removed him from the political arena, and his friends were divided between Mr. Adams and General Jackson. Messrs. Van Buren, Forsyth, and my father, being recognised leaders of the friends of Mr. Crawford who rallied to the support of General Jackson in 1828, all three of them, with Livingston of Louisiana, occupied the chief places in his administration during his eight years in the following order : — 1st, Mr. Van Buren; 2nd, Mr. Livingston; 3rd, Mr. Mc-Lane; 4th, Mr. Forsyth. These four with the Vice-President, Mr. Calhoun, and those already named, may be considered the leaders of the coalition of the Jackson and Crawford parties in 1828, in opposition to the partisans of Mr. Adams and Mr. Clay. Each of these four had contested for the Presidency in 1824 and had been supporters of the Democratic Party under Jefferson, Madison, and Monroe. The Federal Party may be said to have entirely disappeared as a National Party before the close of Mr. Monroe's Administration.

Our political history, however, furnishes no parallel to the partisan violence of the Presidential canvass of 1828, when the candidates were of the same political party. Newspapers in the cities of New York and Philadelphia took the lead in the most atrocious and vulgar abuse of General Jackson, embracing in their vituperation his most private and domestic relations; their example was not without influence upon the press elsewhere, as well as upon individuals. The two honourable gentlemen who were candidates for the Presidency (Mr. Adams and General Jackson) were represented to be infamous and dishonourable—the one a defaulter and a political turncoat—the other an adulterer and a murderer. The truth was that they were both cultivated and gracious gentlemen; the former a scholar and a man of extraordinary experience; the latter a distinguished soldier and a thorough patriot. I will not revive the history of that day by stigmatizing, as they deserve, those who thus abused the liberty of the Press and the freedom of discussion, though I rejoice to note the fact that even in their own day, amid all the partisan passion of the hour, they were estimated at their real value, and rarely succeeded in associating themselves with the leading men of the contending parties. The canvass continued throughout the entire summer of 1828, the friends of General Jackson claiming for him the merit of being an original Jeffersonian Republican, while his tolerant and generous treatment of the Federalists during the administration of Mr. Monroe was presented as an inducement to secure their support against Mr. Adams who had abandoned them at an early day to take service with Mr. Jefferson. These appeals were quite successful, and the Federalists of the Middle States rallied to his standard. I attended one great mass meeting of the citizens of

Maryland and Delaware, which was addressed by my father, General Samuel Smith, and George Read, a grandson of one of the signers of the Declaration of Independence. Other mass meetings were held throughout the country ; in New England, Isaac Hill and Levi Woodbury, both of New Hampshire, conducted the Jackson canvass; in New York Van Buren was the master spirit of the campaign ; in Pennsylvania, Ingham and Buchanan were the chiefs of the original Jackson forces, and General Cass and Colonel Benton in the West. In the South West, Kentucky, under Colonel Richard M. Johnson, F. P. Blair, and Amos Kendal, led the assault upon Mr. Clay who represented the Administration of Mr. Adams. In Tennessee, (Jackson's home), Mississippi, and Louisiana, the enthusiasm of the people was roused to the highest pitch, commencing with a wonderful display on the 8th of January 1828— the anniversary of the battle of New Orleans —and it never abated until the triumphant election of General Jackson gave the people a legitimate satisfaction. In Alabama, Colonel King, afterwards Vice-President, led the canvass. In Georgia, Forsyth and Barrien

5

united the Jackson and Crawford forces. MacDuffie, Hayne, Hamilton and Drayton did the same in South Carolina. Rives and Stevenson led in Virginia, with Branch and Saunders in North Carolina, completing the circuit of victorious States. In 1828 there were 261 electoral votes ; General Jackson received 178, which was a majority, and Mr. Adams received 83.

In a few weeks after the result of the Presidential Election was known at the Hermitage, the name by which General Jackson afterwards came to be generally known, and in the midst of the rejoicing of his near-by friends and neighbours, the great grief of his life fell upon him, in the death of his wife, who had for years been in delicate health. The day of her death—December 22nd, 1828—was one of sorrow and mourning to the people, and to General Jackson one of supreme grief which he bore with him to his grave. Six years later, when I called upon him in Washington to thank him for my appointment as a cadet at West Point, having been invited to breakfast with him I walked from the room in which the sessions of the Cabinet were usually held, into the adjoining one, which was his bed-room. When I perceived the General on his knees I turned promptly to retire, but roused by my step he rose from his kneeling posture and called me by name most affectionately, and taking the miniature of his deceased wife from the table told me she was ever present with him in spirit, and that he always prayed to be united to her in heaven. Perhaps her death was the one event more than any other that ever occurred to tame his fiery nature. Those who knew him intimately all testified to its wonderful effect upon him. I shall never forget myself the touching and noble sorrow with which he referred to her virtuous life and trustful death, and the manly dignity with which he accepted my interruption of his devotions.

I visited my father again in Washington in 1829 to witness the inauguration ot General Jackson, accompanied by my grand-father Colonel Allen McLane, a revolu-tionary soldier who had served under the immediate orders of General Lafayette at the Battle of Brandywine in 1777 as the Com-mander of a troop of horse, and who was subsequently attached to Lee's Legion and served to the end of the war, where he found himself once more under the immediate orders of General Lafayette at the Battle of Yorktown in 1781. He had been appointed by General Washington U. S. Marshal for the District of Delaware, and subsequently Collector of the Port of that district, to which office he had been re-appointed by each successive President from Washington to Adams. He now visited Washington to congratulate General Jackson upon his election, and to receive from him another appointment, which he lived to enjoy only a few months when he died in his 82nd year.

The scene of rejoicing at this inauguration was unexampled in the political history of our country, and the accounts of it from every shade of opinion are most striking. Mr. Webster, in letters to his brother and other friends in New England, represents it as a wonderful demonstration of popular feeling. Unhappily the domestic incidents and personal abuse that characterized the canvass had for its immediate effect the suspension of all courteous intercourse between the incoming and outgoing Executives.

President Adams retired from the White House without receiving the visit of President Jackson, and the latter proceeded to the Capitol on the 4th March without any official attendance, and there took the Oath of Office on the Eastern Portico as administered by the Chief Justice of the United States in the presence of thousands of his delighted and enthusiastic countrymen.

The Cabinet with which he surrounded himself in the Administration of the Government had for its chief Mr. Van Buren of New York, but the Secretaries of the Treasury and Navy, and the Attorney General (Messrs Ingham, Branch, and Barrien) were the devoted friends of the Vice President Mr. Calhoun. The Secretary of War, Mr. Eaton, was the devoted friend of the President himself, and so was the Postmaster-General, Mr. Berry. My father was nominated Minister to England, and in company with Mr. Rives of Virginia, who was nominated Minister to France, left in the United States Frigate " Constellation " early in the same year for their respective posts. Both of them were included in the original cast of the Cabinet, the one as Secretary of the Treasury and the other as Secretary of the Navy, but the influence of the Vice-President and the original friends of General Jackson prevailed in substituting for them respectively Ingham of Pennsylvania and Branch of North Carolina. The influence of the Vice-President who was the recognized Chief of the original friends of General Jackson had prevailed in the organization of the Cabinet, but this success involved intrinsic difficulties and disagreements which resulted in an early estrangement between him and the President. Mr. Forsyth was much more influential in Georgia than Mr. Barrien where Mr. Crawford's friends had complete control of the Democratic Party, and Mr. Buchanan was superior in talent and political consideration to Mr. Ingham in Pennsylvania. In North Carolina, General Saunders was far more in sympathy with the masses of the party than Mr. Branch. These old Crawford men rallied to assert their ascendency, which they did with effect, Mr. Forsyth being soon accepted as a leader in the Senate, and Messrs. Buchanan and Saunders being at no distant day in the front rank of the active partisans of the Administration, while the Vice-President himself with his immediate friends were driven into opposition, and finally into a desperate political antagonism, not only against the President, but against the laws he was sworn to administer. This catastrophe did not occur however, until the Cabinet itself was disorganized and scattered, and a new combination formed to sustain the policy of the Administration and secure the re-election of President Jackson. The summer of 1829 did not pass before the friends who accompanied the President from the West, notably among them W. B. Lewis of Tennessee and Amos Kendal of Kentucky, commenced the canvass which finally separated the President from Mr. Calhoun, and obliged all in and out of the Cabinet to rally to one or other of the political Chieftains. Duff Green, the Editor of the official press of the Administration, was a devoted friend of Mr. Calhoun, and as every member of the Cabinet was obliged to disavow any Presidential aspirations, so this editor was obliged to disavow any intention or wish to present the Vice-President as a a rival to the hero who was now the idol of his party and the country. F. P Blair of Kentucky soon joined his friend Mr. Kendal, and these two experienced and zealous partisans became the master spirits of the Party press throughout the country, and eventually the master spirits of the Administration.

Meanwhile my father and Mr. Rives took passage for Europe on the U. S. Ship of War *Constellation;* my father to enter upon his duties as United States Minister in London, and Mr. Rives to the same post in Paris. On board the *Constellation*—besides my father and Mr. Rives—was Commander Biddle, on his way to command the Mediterranean Fleet. Mr. Rives was accompanied by his wife and children and private secretary, Robert Gilmor. My father had no one with him but Robert Walsh, his private secretary, and myself. Commander Biddle had his private secretary, John Chapman of Philadelphia. This party composed the cabin mess and, under the presiding hospitality of Captain Wadsworth, we had a delightful voyage of thirty days from New York to Cowes. In looking back to this gay and agreeable experience I recall with great pleasure the accomplished gentlemen who constituted the staff of the ship's company, one of them much distinguised throughout his whole professionnal life was an intimate friend of my father—the late Admiral Franklin Buchanan—and another who was my own companion and schoolfellow, midshipman Decatur, nephew of the great naval hero of that name. Buchanan took special care of my father who was a poor sailor, sea-sick throughout the voyage, and grieved greatly in the absence of my mother and his large family who followed him to Europe two months later—the birth of her ninth child, my brother Charles, having rendered necessary this separation. My grandfather's death, early in the same year, contributed to the sadness with which he entered upon his new duties.

A few days on the Isle of Wight refreshed us all, especially my father and Mrs. Rives, who had been ill for thirty days at sea. The latter crossed over to France and we posted to London, where we took up our headquarters at " Thomas' Hotel," Berkeley Square, a most aristocratic Inn from which the " vulgar public " was strictly excluded. The weather was intensely and unusually hot, the whole month of August 1829 being in England a tropical summer. The beautiful London parks, however, were fresh and green, and the nights were comparatively cool. Mr. Washington Irving had arrived from Spain—having left behind him a scorching heat, he found London delightful. Under his auspices it was charming.

He was then at the height of his literary fame, and every one that knew him loved him. He had been many years in Europe, most of the time in England, and accepted the office of Secretary of Legation as a means of returning to his American citizenship; he was proud of his country and proud of his Minister. My father was called on by the chief literary and social magnates of London, and invitations to town and country poured upon him and his secretary. The Duke of Devonshire sent for them to Chatsworth, the most sumptuous and magnificent home in England, and the poets Moore and Rogers, who were intimate friends of Irving, formed there an association with the American Legation which soon ripened into great intimacy. Throughout our residence there Moore's voice and touch at the piano, singing his own songs, constituted one of the greatest attractions at the Legation Receptions. The poet Campbell, the American artists Leslie and Newton were soon added to this charming and charmed circle. Newton fell in love with a sweet American girl, and so did Moore; though the latter was already billetted with as much as he could carry in domestic life. Leslie was married and had a lovely family, and Rogers was loved by every man and woman who knew him. It is impossible to express how much prestige this literary circle, of which Mr. Irving was the centre, gave to the American Legation in Society; American beauty was then, as now, very conspicuous. Lady Wellesley was perhaps the most distinguished of this circle, she was living with her sister, Miss Caton, in a Regent's Park Villa, and there was a close intimacy between that family and the Legation during our stay in London. The Duke of Wellington was very fond of his sister-in-law, and the gossip of that day was that she was Marchioness of Wellesley because there was already a Duchess of Wellington. The single sister, Miss Betsy Caton, had been a close friend of my mother from girlhood ; this intercourse constituted a charming incident in our life in London. My mother came out from America in October 1829, and by her presence and tact she rendered the house in Chandos Street, where my father had established the Legation, one of the most agreeable in London. She had been my father's constant companion for more than twenty years in political life in Washington, and as she was his principal and only support in domestic life and happiness so was she his best support in political life, and notably during the two periods when he was U.S. Minister to London. In 1829, under General Jackson, and again in 1845 under Mr. Polk : at both of these periods the same public men were in power in England, to wit :—Wellington, Aberdeen, and Peel ; and with them at each of these periods he was successful in consummating the object of his mission to the satisfaction of his Government and countrymen.

The immediate object of his mission in

1829 was to obtain from Great Britain the privilege for American vessels to enter and trade at their Colonial ports. This privilege we had never fully possessed since our colonial days, and sundry retaliatory statutes had been enacted by the United States. The object of the mission was fully and satisfactorily accomplished by an agreement in the nature of a treaty, though not technically such. This agreement was that Congress should empower the President whenever he should be satisfied that England would open to us her Colonial ports, to proclaim our own ports open to British vessels with the repeal of the laws of 1818, 1820, and 1828. Congress authorized the President in 1830 to issue such a proclamation, and in October 1830 he did so issue it, thus restoring to American vessels the privilege of trading in all the British Colonial ports.

Prior to my mother's arrival I was rather a boss in the household of Chandos Street, the Legation alone on the first floor being independent of my authority. Mr. Irving thought it dreadful to see a youth just rid of his round-about taking charge of an English butler and ordering dinner. My father however was no housekeeper, and as he and I constituted the family, he was delighted to leave me entire liberty. We breakfasted early—lunched at 12, and dined at 8 p.m. Irving, who lived near by, generally came into dinner, and neither he nor Mr. Walsh ever complained of the "good cheer" we furnished them. We had friends almost every day, but once a week a dinner. Mr. Irving's circle of literary men always furnished a fair proportion of guests, and though he hated boys as much as he loved girls, we managed to keep the peace and be good friends. Nevertheless it nearly set him wild that my father allowed me to ride a pony daily to Brompton, where I went every morning to school. I returned in the early afternoon, and always galloped through Hyde Park at the height of fashion's hour.

I saw a great deal of the Bates family (the American branch of the house of Baring), the son was just my age, and the daughter a year younger, was beautiful. Naturally it was easy to fall in love with her, and when I did this Mr. Irving set it down as another boyish outrage. He was an old bachelor about whom several romantic love stories were told, but no one ever knew his sweet heart. This young lady in due time escaped from my boyish passion, and married Mr. Van der Meyer, the Belgian Minister, and was in due time the intimate friend of Queen Victoria; the relations between the English and Belgian Courts being very intimate. King Leopold was in fact the Mentor of the Queen. Mr. Bates was a very close friend of my father, and remarkably well informed upon all questions, and of the more domestic features of English social life.

At this period English Social Life was not very nice—the King (George IV.) was an old rake and *roué* whose manhood was pretty well exhausted. Whether at St. James' in London, or at Windsor, was all the same —no one but the Duke of Wellington was able to impress him with any respect for his Official State and his Public Duties. His Royal brothers held high places in the State and lived scandalous and worthless lives, entirely inconsistent with their rank and station.

Princess Victoria lived with her mother at Kensington Palace, and was a girl of an attractive disposition, but rarely ever seen in public, and the Duchess had no intercourse with her uncles or with general society, so that whatever demoralisation society at large experienced from the low life of the Royal Dukes, the domestic circle of the future Queen was protected. The Duke of Clarence, who was an Admiral in the Navy and was to succeed George IV. as King, had a family of bastards who were living pensioned upon the State and Society. The Duke of Cumberland was a dissolute and dangerous character whose presence was not permitted in any well ordered family in England. The Dukes of Gloucester and Sussex were weak, almost insignificant in personal consideration, though not so dissolute as the others: on the whole however, the Royal Family was very low, and when they were not bad they were crazy! The public press and caricature shops of London did not spare them, but lampooned them without measure, and it seemed impossible at times to administer decently the Government with such an Executive ; for the King being subject to fits of passion and caprice reasonable intercourse with him was impossible. All this of course had great influence upon Society, and tended greatly to discredit aristocratic institutions and families. The spirit of reform extended itself in every direction, and in a very few years not only was the suffrage greatly extended, but the Government of England was largely transferred to those who had sprung from the middle classes, and though the form of Government was not changed the popular element was greatly reinforced.

During this reign and the following or William IV. the Duke of Wellington was a sort of guardian angel for the Monarchy; he, and he alone, could preserve decent intercourse with the King. After the death of George IV. Lord Grey and the party of reform found it well nigh impossible to perform their Constitutional duties with the Sovereign. But whether in or out of office the presence and influence of the Duke— sometimes called " King Arthur " — was always at hand to preserve peace and order. In the midst of this interesting period, after Christmas 1829, I left London and passed the year 1830 in Paris; a period not less uninteresting on the continent, socially and politically, than it was in London.

I left London the day after Christmas with Mr. Jonathan Amory of Boston; we posted to Dover, and crossing the Channel to Calais, we posted thence to Paris, where we took lodgings at Meurice's Hotel, Rue de Rivoli, the 29th December 1829. We left the political world in England much disturbed—the King and Court constantly in conflict with parliamentary government. The death of Canning left the Tories without a leader of intellectual force, and but for the prestige of the Duke of Wellington the reform element would have taken possession of the Government, and the wildest spirit of democracy would have prevailed: as it was the Tories held possession of the Government until the death of the King, and for a little while under his successor. In France the struggle that Charles X. had maintained for five years against the popular will and the legal operation of constitutional government was tottering to its fall, and from January 1830 to the three glorious days of July the triumph of liberal principles was imminent.

The French King was a gentleman perfectly devoted to the principle of Royal privilege and sovereignty, with no toleration for the "Bourgeoisie" who constituted the main element of opposition to his government, though he manifested kind feeling for the common people. His immediate friends, public and private, shared these absolute opinions in all domestic politics, and in foreign affairs he had cultivated the intimacy and friendship of Russia. This naturally put him in conflict with England, and rendered very difficult the support and application of a liberal policy in the administration of his Government. His Prime Minister, Prince Polignac, was more absolute in temper than the King himself, and after a struggle of years maintained with the Chiefs of the Constitutional Party, such as Thiers, Guizot, Odillon Barrot, Lafitte, Casimir Perier, and the like, he threw away all reserve and moderation dissolved the Parliament and destroyed the electoral franchise, the liberty of the Press and speech. The actual climax was not reached until the month of July 1830, but throughout the first six months of the year this catastrophe might have been expected at any day or any hour; if it did not occur sooner it was due to the indifference of the common people and the caution of the " Bourgeoisie" and their constitutional chieftains.

Paris in January 1830 was, to the eye of the stranger, as beautiful as it had ever been. The Army was commanded by the Marshals and Generals of the Empire, and a review of twenty-five thousand men on the Champ de Mars by Charles X was imposing ; while the ball at the Palais Royal given to the King of Naples in the month of May which was attended by King Charles X was more splendid than any ever given after 1830 at the Tuileries by Louis Philippe or Louis Napoleon.

The first visit I made in Paris was to Mr. Rives and Mr. Harper, our Minister and Secretary of Legation. The second was to General Lafayette, who was my grandfather's friend and companion in arms.

Mr. and Mrs. Rives received me kindly, our voyage from the United States on the " Constellation" having established relations of cordial friendship between us. Mr.

Harper, who lived close by the Hotel Meurice in the rue Castiglione, gave me an introduction to the tutor of his brother Robert, Mr. Gustave Lemoine, and took an apartment for me opposite his hotel in the rue Castiglione, and in a few weeks arranged for me to be domiciled with his brother in the Pension Garbaux, where we had rooms adjoining our tutor, Here I entered upon my course of study of French, and with the pupils of the Pension Garbaux I followed the classes in the Collège Bourbon.

General Lafayette approved and advised these arrangements, and I was most enthusiastic in the pursuit of this course of study which combined great personal liberty with the best possible instruction. Mr. Lemoine was a charming companion and a cultivated scholar. He prepared me in all my college courses and gave me special instruction in French, and we were daily companions for the afternoons and evenings, several of which in each week we passed at the Théâtre Francais, where his brother, subsequently Directeur of the Théâtre du Gymnase, was a principal actor. Under his direction I was prepared for my college classes and rapidly acquired familiarity with the French language. Jules Lasteyrie, the grandson of Lafayette, became one of my constant companions, he and his younger brother Ferdinand (who afterwards married in America Miss Seabrook of Hilton Head, South Carolina) became my intimate friends, and years afterwards in America, when I was an officer in the Army, I received Ferdinand in Florida, and he accompanied me to General Taylor's Head Quarters.

The year 1830 was in France a year of extraordinary excitement with wonderful results. The first half of the year saw the effort of the King and his Ministers to restore absolutism to the Monarchy, which culminated in the month of July with the publication of the Royal Decrees or "Ordonnances" that dissolved the Chambers and suspended the freedom of the Press. Members of the Chamber thus violently dispossessed of their representative character, and the editors of all the principal journals of Paris replied to these decrees with counter proclamations. An indescribable alarm took possession of all the trading and commercial classes; in public and private assemblies the decress were denounced. For several days this form of opposition and defiance was all that could be observed.

Little by little the excitement reached the common people, and the public meetings became disorderly. During the day and night of the 27th and 28th July several collisions occurred between the people, the police, and some military detachments; but the storm reached its height with furious fighting on the 29th and 30th July. The Monarchy was overthrown by the 31st. On the 28th, the people surrounded the Collège Bourbon and tore down the Royal "Fleur de Lys" that decorated its walls. Instead of returning to the Pension Garbaux after the college classes were dismissed I went to Mr. Harper's in the Rue Castiglione, where I passed the night. That section of the city was comparatively quiet, the troops having possession of the Rue de Rivoli, the Place Vendôme, the Place de la Concorde, the Tuileries and the Louvre, but all the city to the North and East was in possession of the insurgents, and the troops had already in many sections refused to fire upon them.

They defended themselves from the windows and roofs of the houses, and from behind the barricades hurriedly erected in all the principal thoroughfares. The following day the fighting continued, but everywhere the troops were giving way, and the people commanded by young soldiers of the Polytechnic School and adventurers who sprang into life at the moment, were gaining ground. Lafayette was the only commanding figure in this revolution, the people who did the fighting came slowly into action without leaders and without cordial sympathy for the "Bourgeoisie" or the men of letters and the journalists who had conducted the political and parliamentary opposition that terminated what are still known as the three bloody days of July. Indeed the leaders of this opposition were unequal to the great opportunity they had created, and instead of founding a Republic they were afraid to assume even temporary power. Lafitte, Casimir Perier, Thiers, and all such were halting, and hesitating, and intriguing with the partisans of the Duke of Orleans for the establishment of a Regency or another Monarchy. Lafayette alone—serene and brave

—was equal to the occasion, and accepted the command of the National Guard which, when the storm was at its height on the 29th July, represented all that existed of government and authority. He was beloved by the people and respected by the Bourgeoisie. In truth, at this moment, all deferred to him, Bankers, Deputies, and Nobles (the Duke of Orleans included) recognised him as the chieftain of the hour. With his nephew Lasteyrie I accompanied him to the Hotel de Ville on the 29th of July, where he received the Duke of Orleans, and on the following day—the 30th of July I think it was—I accompanied him to the Palais Royal when, in the presence of thousands, he proclaimed the Duke *Lieutenant-General*. Most of the Republicans grieved at this termination of the strife, but Lafayette, a true patriot, loving his country, saw no other solution but bloodshed and anarchy. He was literally the saviour of his country, and he remained its guardian angel and anchor of safety throughout the year 1830. At its close Louis Philippe, consolidated in his power as King, with Parliamentary Ministers as his Counsellors, was not unwilling to be emancipated from his control. Lafayette then resigned the command of the National Guard and returned to private life. These reminiscences are not history, but I venture little when I note here that, but for the virtue and courage of Lafayette, the King and Court as well as the Duke of Orleans and his sons would all have been slaughtered, and France itself surrendered to Anarchy and violence such as befel her in the Revolution of 1789.

In January 1831 I returned to London. King William IV had succeeded to the throne. The political condition of England was still agitated. The Tory party was discredited; Earl Grey was recognized as the chief of the Reform party consisting of the Whigs and their new allies, prominent Liberals conspicuous in the Reform agitation. My father had been very successful in his mission and had contracted a warm friendship with the Chiefs of the Tory Party, with whom he had concluded the commercial arrangement that opened to the commerce of the United States the Colonial ports of Great Britain. Whatever may have been his political sympathy with the Reform Agitation, he never dissembled his regard for the Duke of Wellington, Lord Aberdeen, and Sir Robert Peel. The Reform Ministry however was in possession of the Government, and new men dominated in English politics before he left England, which he did in the summer of 1831, to assume the duties of Secretary of the Treasury in the Second Cabinet of General Jackson.

We returned to the United States in August, having been just two years in England, two years most agreeably spent, my sister Rebecca (Mrs. Philip Hamilton) being the only one of twelve children in Society. She was very clever, with fine tastes and an accomplished musician. She was the centre of a charming circle of young people, Miss Matilda Carter (afterwards Mrs. Willing) being one of its great attractions. When I returned from Paris, though only in my sixteenth year, I aspired to be received in it, and I had a terrible scene with Mr. Irving because I refused to wear a round-about at the Birth-Night Ball of Princess Victoria. I prevailed however, being well supported by my sister and Miss Carter, the

latter asking nothing better than to add a
boy of sixteen to her string of admirers old
and young—for she already had them of
every age—Tom Moore and the venerable
poet Rogers included. At the Ball, notwithstanding my dress coat of the latest Parisian
fashion, I was seated at the foot of the
Throne on which sat William IV and
his Queen, with the sons of the foreign
Ambassadors and Ministers to take their turn
in the quadrilles in which the Princess was
to dance. Her partners were the Princes
George of Cumberland and Cambridge. The
son of Prince Esterhazy, Austrian Ambassador, was the only partner with whom she
danced other than her two cousins. The
only one of the three now living is the
Duke of Cambridge. The Princess was a
lovely little girl, the present Prince of Wales
is her perfect image. This Birth-Night Ball,
and a visit to the Highlands of Scotland and
the Isle of Man with the Duke of Argyle,
are the only incidents of any social note that
I have to recall of my second visit to England. Sir Fitzroy MacLean accompanied
my father from Castle Inverary to the Isle of
Man, to which the Clan of MacLean had

retired, and from which my great grandfather emigrated to Ireland in 1731, and thence to America (Philadelphia), where my grandfather was born. It was he who changed the spelling of his name from McLean to McLane, because, as the legend goes, there was an officer in the British Army during the Revolutionary War who bore the family name and spelled it as our ancestor had done. They were in the opposing armies at the Battle of Germantown.

My grandfather went into business with Robert Morris in the three lower counties of Delaware in 1773, where he was living when the War of the Revolution called him to arms, and with his own means he organised a troop of horse which constituted a partisan corps in the Army of General Washington before Philadelphia, and in command of which he subsequently joined "Lee's Legion."

We reached the United States on our return in August 1831. My father went at once to Washington and I accompanied him. He took charge of the Treasury Department immediately, leaving his family in Delaware. General Jackson never had an hour of peace or satisfaction with his first Cabinet. It had been organised under the influence of the Vice-President, Mr. Calhoun, and from its origin it was distracted by the intrigues of those who desired to maintain the influence of the Vice-President, and make him the successor of General Jackson. The special friends of the President resented this, and determined to make an issue with the Vice-President. Domestic and social differences greatly aggravated the quarrel. The friends of Mr. Crawford who had always been hostile to the Vice-President took a conspicuous part in the controversy, and Mr. Crawford himself, who had been Mr. Calhoun's colleague in the Cabinet of Mr. Monroe, was cited as authority for the allegation that Mr. Calhoun had been hostile to General Jackson when his military conduct was arraigned under that administration. As Mr. Calhoun had always professed friendship for General Jackson, he was now reproached with hypocrisy and deceit; crimination and recrimination between himself and General Jackson followed, resulting in a complete rupture of the friendly relations which had existed between them. The Secretaries of the Treasury and Navy and the

Attorney General espoused the cause of Mr. Calhoun, while the immediate friends of General Jackson, with the Secretary of War and the Postmaster General, professed to believe that Mr. Calhoun had acted unworthily. They were sustained by General Jackson's friends outside of the Cabinet, notably by Messrs. W. B. Lewis and Amos Kendal. All the leading Crawford men in the Southern States took sides against Mr. Calhoun. The party was thus distracted and disorganised when Congress met, and the friends of Mr. Calhoun, including General Duff Green, the Editor of the Administration organ, *The Washington Telegraph*, determined to sustain him as the Democratic Candidate for the Vice-Presidency, and if necessary for the Presidency itself. The feud increased during the Session of Congress, and before the end of the Session the breach was irreparable. Meanwhile the families of the three Secretaries who were attached to Mr. Calhoun refused to associate with the wife of the Secretary of War (Mrs. Eaton), and a social war was inaugurated against this lady. She was reported to have been too "intimate" with her husband before marriage. He was married just before the Cabinet was organised, and no sooner was the political incident to which I have referred manifested, than the social incident was connected with it. This latter was far more active in making life unpleasant in administration circles than the former—between the two it became unsupportable. The Secretary of State was the only stranger to the quarrel—he was a bachelor and it cost him nothing to maintain courteous intercourse with the family of the Secretary of War. In accepting the office of Secretary of State he had disclaimed all Presidential aspirations for himself, and he very soon announced himself in favour of the renomination of General Jackson, and as opposed to the one term principle to which it was said the President had pledged himself. This feud continued through the year 1830, and in the spring of 1831 it may be said the Cabinet was dissolved. Edward Livingston of Louisiana, a devoted friend of the President, had been selected as Secretary of State, as Mr. Van Buren had been the first to resign, recognising the impossibility of maintaining the old organisation of the Cabinet. My father had been selected as

Secretary of the Treasury; General Cass, Governor of Michigan, as Secretary of War; Levi Woodbury, Secretary of the Navy; R. B. Taney, Attorney General; and the Postmaster General, Mr. Barry, was to remain. This arrangement left out the three friends of Mr. Calhoun. My father and Mr. Livingston had been originally desired by General Jackson for the posts to which they were now appointed. It may be said the entire Cabinet was perfectly free and independent of all the social and all the political differences which the feud in the first Cabinet had engendered, though they were all influential members of the party. They were all unanimously confirmed by the Senate, and there was a reasonable hope that the party might recover its harmony; but Congress had not been long in Session before the violent personalities which had destroyed the first Cabinet found occasion to break forth again; and when the Senate came to the consideration of Mr. Van Buren's nomination as Minister to England, it was discovered that Mr. Calhoun had united with Mr. Webster and the leaders of the Opposition in a determination to reject him. This was done by the casting vote of the Vice-President, and from that moment Mr. Van Buren was the recognised favourite of the Administration for the Vice-Presidency. In the summer of 1832 he was nominated to that office, and elected to it on the ticket with General Jackson in November of that year, Mr. Calhoun himself being thenceforth in opposition.

The happy influence of the new Cabinet was perceptible in its spirit of union and harmony, socially as well as politically, and during the Session of Congress that preceded the Presidential Election General Jackson, in his Message to Congress, left the Bank question to the best judgment of Congress. The Secretary of the Treasury, Mr. McLane, without giving sanction to the political bias of the existing bank sustained its constitutionality, and enforced strongly the necessity for a fiscal agent of the Government: he set forth in clear and practical form the principle of a revenue tariff with incidental protection within the revenue limit to American industry. He framed a Bill on these principles in response to a call by the House of Representatives. There was already pending in the House a

Tariff Bill prepared by **Mr. MacDuffie**, Chairman of the Committee of Ways and Means, and later on Mr. John Quincy Adams reported another Bill from the Committee on Manufactures. The consideration of these Bills led to a very full debate in which the Revenue and protective principles were discussed, but the Bill adopted by the House did not settle the controversy or give a victory to either side, so that the question constituted an issue in the Presidential canvass, and later on gave rise to the movement in South Carolina to nullify the law passed by Congress. Mr. Clay was the great champion of protection; Mr. Calhoun was the father of nullification, while General Jackson adhered to the principle of a revenue tariff and the perpetuation of the Union. Mr. Clay became the champion too of the Bank of the United States as a Political Bank under the direction of his own friend and partisan Mr. Biddle. Naturally enough General Jackson, who was well disposed to re-charter the Bank as an independent fiscal agent of the Treasury, was soon involved in a relentless war against the existing Bank, identified as it was with his immediate political opponents.

Political parties were greatly divided upon

these two great issues when the Presidential canvass of 1832 commenced. General Jackson himself was a revenue tariff statesman, moderate and reasonable in his views. Mr. Clay and Mr. Calhoun stood forth as the champions of the two extreme views, neither of which had ever prevailed. But for the courage and patriotism of Jackson civil war and bloodshed would have caused the desolation of South Carolina under the leadership of Mr. Calhoun. In reference to the Bank General Jackson had in his intimate circle of friends some of its strong and earnest opponents, notably Mr. Amos Kendal and Mr. F. P. Blair of Kentucky, and Mr. Hill of New Hampshire; but he had been in no great degree hostile to its re-charter with some modifications, and he was supported in this view by his principal Cabinet Ministers, notably by Messrs. Livingston, McLane, and Cass. All such difference of opinion disappeared however in the face of the partisan conduct of the Bank which had united its fortunes with the Presidential Candidature of Mr. Clay, who pressed forward the Bill for its re-charter which was passed by Congress, and was vetoed by the President in the summer of 1832. This veto was the proclamation of the Democratic Party against the party of privilege and class legislation then being organized by Mr. Clay.

Col. Benton was the giant in this debate on the veto of the Bank. Mr. Webster, Mr. Clay, Mr. Dallas, and Mr. Clayton were all arrayed against him, but they were all worsted, and though they had the majority of the Senate, the country did not sustain them. The Veto Message itself was a powerful paper, and asserted the popular doctrine of the early Democracy. Equal rights against Monopoly and class legislation — it conceding that distinctions in Society will always exist, and that " equality of talents, of education, or of wealth, cannot be produced by human institutions " — claiming that " in the full enjoyment of the gifts of heaven and the fruits of industry, economy, and virtue, every man is entitled to protection by law". It also asserted the grand principle that the laws should not add to these natural and just advantages artificial distinctions or grand titles, gratuitous and exclusive privileges to make the rich richer, and the potent more powerful — " that Government should confine itself to equal protection, and as heaven does its rains, shower its fruits alike on the high and the low, the rich and the poor". In the debate Colonel Benton was in violent antagonism to Mr. Clay; they gave each other the lie in as plain terms as parliamentary forms and language would permit; the one revived the old scandal of bargain and corruption between Messrs. Clay and Adams, and the other brought to light all the violent denunciation of General Jackson indulged in by Colonel Benton in 1824. Both were obliged to apologize to the Senate for the violence and indecorum of their speeches.

The result of the Presidential election was the triumphant success of General Jackson, who received 219 electoral votes against 44 cast for Mr. Clay. When Congress met, the policy of General Jackson was set forth in his Annual Message of December 1832 with great vigour and clearness, the principle of a revenue tariff being sustained, and the United States Bank vigorously condemned.

Soon afterwards the President issued a Proclamation in defence of the Union and the supremacy of the law. As early as December 13th, the Senate requested the Secretary of the Treasury to propose a Revenue Tariff Bill. The Ways and Means

Committee in the House reported in the same month a Bill drawn up in conformity with the Secretary's views, which proposed a great reduction of taxes. In January the President reported to Congress the nullification proceedings in South Carolina, and requested new power for the Executive to collect revenue by military force if necessary, and execute the laws upon individuals with necessary legal processes from the United States Court. This Force Message was originally prepared by the Secretary of the Treasury as a Treasury report, and adopted by the President as a Message which, with the proclamation drafted by Mr. Livingston, set forth the policy of the Administration. A great debate followed on all the Constitutional points involved, and the triumph of the Administration was complete. A most effective Force Bill was enacted, and Mr. Clay abandoned his protective policy, and introduced in the Senate February 12th. what he called a Compromise Tariff Bill, which superseded the Revenue Tariff Bill prepared by the Secretary of the Treasury. It provided that all the duties which were over twenty per cent should be reduced one tenth of the excess over twenty per cent after September 1835, and one tenth each alternate year afterwards until 1841, then one half the remaining excess should be repealed, and in 1842 the tax should be twenty per cent horizontal with a good free list and valuation. Mr. Calhoun accepted the compromise. For years afterwards they each contended that they had not abandoned their principles; Mr. Clay professing he had saved the American system and policy of protection, while Mr. Calhoun insisted that the Compromise Bill was the triumph of the principle of Free Trade.

This coalition of Mr. Clay and Mr. Calhoun in passing the Compromise Bill to defeat the intelligent revenue project of the Administration was considered a very lame and impotent conclusion for two such statesmen, and as the Force Bill, recommended by the President, passed almost simultaneously with it General Jackson and his Administration obtained great prestige, while his political opponents were greatly discredited. Mr. Clay was left in an awkward extremity as the Protectionists would not listen to reason, and still less to Mr. Calhoun, and had no alternative but submission to the

Compromise Bill or the policy of the Administration.

The Tariff controversy was settled by the passage of the Compromise Bill, but the war with the Bank of the United States continued and it was proposed that Congress should provide for the withdrawal of the public deposits from the Bank. The majority of the House of Representatives however opposed this policy, and the President was urged by the extreme opponents of the Bank to withdraw the deposits on his own responsibility. Excited to the highest pitch of resentment he was well disposed to do so. As long as my father remained Secretary of the Treasury he was able to control the policy of the Administration which was to leave the public deposits in the Bank until Congress should provide by law for the safe keeping thereof in the Treasury ; but he was transferred to the State Department in the place of Mr. Livingston, who was appointed Minister to France. The difficulties which Mr. Biddle opposed to the payment of the National Debt, and the unfriendly and illegal conduct of the Bank in reference to the protested drafts of the Government on France for the first instalment or the French indemnity under the Treaty of French Spoliation Claims, fairly exasperated the President and encouraged him to take the responsibility of removing the deposits by an executive order. Mr. Taney, the Attorney General, was the only member of the Cabinet who supported this policy. After much discussion in the Cabinet and in Congress this view prevailed. Mr. Duane, who had been appointed Secretary of the Treasury, refused to obey the orders of the President to make the removal. He was removed, and Mr. Taney was appointed Secretary of the Treasury with the understanding that he would do so, which he did in conformity with the President's wishes. Messrs. Kendall and F. P. Blair were recognized as the tried advocates of this policy in the inner circle of the President's friends, with Messrs. Benton and Hill in the Senate to support them. The Vice-President, Mr. Van Buren, and all the other members of the Cabinet had preferred to await the enactment of a law to authorize the removal and provide for the safe keeping of the public money, but Congress would not pass any such law, and most of them yielded a reluctant assent to the President's independent action.

Throughout the summer of 1833 this strife continued, and negotiations went on with the State Banks for the safe keeping of the public money until the 18th of September, when the President settled the question by reading to his Cabinet a paper announcing his determination to remove the deposits.

The Senate, by resolution, denounced the President's policy as unconstitutional, and rejected the nomination of Mr. Taney as Secretary of the Treasury and afterwards as Judge of the Supreme Court for the Maryland District. The House of Representatives concurred with the Senate in its disapproval of the President's Policy, but in the new Congress the Senate and House of Representatives sustained the President. Mr. Taney was nominated by the President as Chief Justice of the United States and confirmed by the Senate, and in March 1834 Mr. Polk reported to the House of Representatives resolutions in full support of the President, which were adopted by a large majority.

Mr. Polk's resolution covered four points. 1st. That the Bank ought not to be rechartered. 2nd. That the deposits ought not to be restored. 3rd. That the State

Banks ought to be depositories of the public money. 4th. That a Committee of Inquiry should be appointed on the Bank. When these resolutions were accepted and adopted by the President as the Programme of his Administration, my father determined that it was his duty to himself and the President to resign as Secretary of State. His relations with the President were of the most intimate character, personal and political. On his return from England in 1831 the President and himself were in perfect accord, they were agreed that the Bank should be re-chartered but modified in its functions, and constituted a fiscal agent of the Government under official control and entirely independent of party politics. The President's Message and the Report of the Secretary of the Treasury were received with great satisfaction by the country, and clearly manifested the reasonable views of the Executive; the Bank nevertheless persisted in its partisan association, and the Secretary of the Treasury fully supported the President in his resolution to veto the Bank Bill as passed by Congress in 1832; but he resisted the extreme opponents of the Bank who urged upon the President the immediate removal of the deposits to the State Banks. He insisted that all the evils which had been experienced from this misconduct and misuse of the public money by the Bank of the United States would be a hundred fold greater if this transfer were made.

In the summer of 1833 Mr. Mc Lane was the only member of the Cabinet who advised the President in writing to await Congressional action and not to transfer by his own acts the public money to the State Banks. General Cass concurred verbally with him, and both of them proposed to resign when the President in September took the responsibility of making the transfer. Major W. B. Lewis, the intimate friend of the President, intervened, and at the request of the President they consented to remain, each reserving his entire independence of opinion.

My father consented to remain that he might give his influence and assistance to those friends of the President who desired the enactment of a law for the establishment of an institution or fiscal agent for the permanent safe keeping and disbursement of the public money. The adoption of Mr. Polk's

49

resolutions united the party on this issue however, and as my father had predicted ruinous speculations and Bank disaster as the consequence thereof, he insisted with the President that it was his duty to resign. The President reluctantly accepted this view, and published his correspondence with my father, who resigned before the adjournment of Congress, without in any way disturbing his relations of friendship with the President.

With some other friends, however, in the party his withdrawal from the Cabinet occasioned very disagreeable incidents. The earnest advocates of the policy of immediate removal were delighted to have Mr. Mc Lane leave the Cabinet, and they did the best to break the effect of his withdrawal by representing it as a political defection. The party at large, however, fully appreciated his course, and the prompt fulfilment of his prediction of the failure of the State Banks increased the respect they entertained for his good judgment. Mr. Polk, whose resolutions were the immediate occasion of his withdrawal from General Jackson's Cabinet, appointed him Minister to England, when he was elected President in 1844, and subsequently invited him to be Secretary of State in place of Mr. Buchanan, who desired to be transferrred to the U.S. Supreme Court. Mr. McLane declined the appointment, preferring to remain in private life. He was then President of the B. and O. Railroad Company, and he had accepted from that company a leave of absence to fill the mission to England pending the negotiation of the Oregon boundary. He had previously declined to enter political life in opposition to the Democratic Party.

My father left Washington in the summer of 1834, immediately after the adjournment of Congress, and returned to Delaware. I accompanied him to New York in the early summer, being on furlough from West Point. I had been appointed a cadet by General Jackson, and had just passed my examination of the first year's studies. I graduated three years later, in 1837, and was commissioned in the 1st Regiment of the U.S. Artillery.

In New York, my father accepted the Presidency of the Morris Canal and Banking Company, and the family moved to New York where they resided until 1837, when he was appointed President of the Baltimore

and Ohio Railroad Company, and removed to Maryland.

We had all enjoyed our residence in Washington. The President's family consisted of his nephew, Andrew Jackson Donelson with his lovely wife, and three young ladies from Tennessee. They constituted a very gay circle, and night after night the General sat in the chimney corner of the parlor that adjoins the dining room, smoking his clay pipe. Music enlivened the evenings, and always " Home, Sweet Home " and "Auld Lang Syne " were given for the General. Mr. Livingston's family consisted of his wife and daughter and a lovely girl, Miss Carleton, niece of Mr. Livingston. The families of General Cass, Mr. Woodbury, and Mr. Taney were all intimate with each other, and Washington Society was never more brilliant than at that period; though I was not there continuously, being still at my studies at Pittfield, Massachusets, I found friendship in the families of General Cass, Mr. Woodbury and Mr. Taney, which have been uninterrupted through my whole life. To General Jackson himself I am not only indebted for my appointment as a cadet, but it was to his influence and encouragement I am indebted for continuing there until my graduation. I disliked more than I can express the confinement and discipline of that institution, and twice during my term there I resigned, and each time it was due to his wishes alone that I consented to remain.

He was very kind to young people, and to me he had an affectionate address which inspired great confidence and devotion. He was very fond of the "Saddle" and whenever I was in Washington I had his permission to join his suite which consisted generally of Major Lewis, whose daughter was generally of the party, and his private secretary, Mr. Donelson. I had a first class mount, a John Richard colt that my father gave me when he was three years old, a wonderful horse to gallop and leap. I trained him to leap almost any length, and safely to go over any ordinary post and rail fence. The delight of the General was to see me give him this exercise. This horse, "Tom Breeze," was the best saddle horse I ever knew. After I graduated at West Point he was my saddle horse for several winters, when fox-hunting was the fashion, and no match for him ever appeared.

53

He was a dark bay of beautiful form, cut up a little too high behind, giving him very long hind legs, to which was due his wonderful power in leaping; he had no trot, but his gallop was a natural gait that went easily up from five miles an hour to ten, which latter pace he could hold for four or five hours continuously.

The four years at West Point were not very interesting to me; the summer of 1834 I passed with my father at Brandywine Springs and in New York, and I had another furlough in 1836 when I visited Washington for a few days and took leave of General Jackson. It was the year of the Presidential Election when Mr. Van Buren was elected President. My intimacy with the President's family had not been affected by my father's retirement from public life. Indeed his retirement had always been a source of regret to the President, and though his war against the Bank still continued his master passion in politics, many events had occurred to make him regret his separation from one who had been his chief, if not his favourite counsellor, in his second Presidential canvass, and in his great struggle with the combined forces of Messrs. Clay and Calhoun in 1832-33.

General Jackson had expressed to Colonel King, the Senator from Alabama, an intimate friend of my father, his desire to effect a reconciliation between my father and Mr. Van Buren. They had never met since the summer of 1833 when they separated in New York at the time General Jackson passed through that city on his visit to Boston. It was at this time that Mr. Van Buren determined to acquiesce in General Jackson's desire to transfer the deposits from the Bank of the United States to the State Banks. The relations between them for many years had been very close and they were in entire accord as to the impolicy of the proposed change. They had agreed in supporting the President's veto of the Bank in 1832, and in recommending Congressional legislation for the safe keeping of the public money. This intimacy and concurrence of opinion made the separation more embarrassing than it would have been under ordinary circumstances, and my father was persuadnd that Mr. Van Buren still regarded the change as unwise and injurious to the public interest.

They parted in New York after a conference in which this difference of views was recognised, and my father returned to Washington. Colonel King was not successful in his mediation, and my father authorised me in my conversation with General Jackson, should he refer to the subject, to tell him he regretted he could not associate himself with him in his efforts to elect Mr. Van Buren, and that he remained of the opinion that we had already experienced the first evil effect of the new policy in extraordinary Bank speculation and inflation, and that we would next experience the reaction in the bankruptcy and ruin of Banks and individuals. I told General Jackson all this and more, and I told him further that my father would not vote for Mr. Van Buren, whose administration he believed would experience this ruin, and be obliged to seek Congressional legislation to provide for the safe keeping of the public money. Although the General was not very gracious to those who opposed his wishes, he concluded this interview with most affectionate greetings to my father. Nothing in our political history is more remarkable than the ultimate failure of this fiscal policy of General Jackson which culminated during Mr. Van Buren's Administration and overwhelmed it with disaster and defeat. I communicated to Colonel King my conversation with General Jackson, and it was by him repeated to Mr. Van Buren. The separation between them was very painful to many mutual friends who had been intimately associated with them in the Crawford campaign of 1824, and in the organisation of the Jackson Party in 1828.

The delight of a Cadet on his graduation is supreme! Yet he is not long in the world without regretting the charm of the intimacy which united him with his friends at the Military Academy. In my own case I formed friendships there which accompanied me through life. Randolph Ridgely of Maryland, Joseph R. Anderson of Virginia, Alexander Macomb of the District of Columbia, Harry Turner of Virginia, Montgomery Meigs of Pennsylvania, and Alexander Hamilton of New York were of my most intimate circle, and at different times my room mates. They were all distinguished in their career at West Point, and several of them in their subsequent career in the

Army. I went at once to Washington on leaving West Point, and thence to Fortress Monroe, where some thousands of recruits had been collected for service in Florida, and the entire class of 1837 was ordered there from West Point to prepare them for the regiments at the seat of war. In Washington I found the political world in great trouble ; the State Banks throughout the country had suspended their payments, and bankruptcy prevailed in all industrial pursuits. The Administration was endeavouring to maintain specie payments, but the effort was a failure, as the Banks had loaned the public money to speculators who declared themselves bankrupts whenever the Banks called in their loans. The distribution of the surplus money as ordered by Congress in the previous year, and the Specie Circular of the Treasury Department intensified the crisis, and completed the disastrous reaction which followed the fictitious prosperity produced by the Bank expansion that ensued on the transfer of the public money from the United States Bank to the State Banks. Mr. Van Buren met the crisis with great courage and self control. He declared that the

Government was in no wise responsible for the misconduct of the State Banks, and he called a Special Session of the new Congress to provide for the safe keeping of the public money in the Treasury, and for its distribution, as well as its collection, in specie. This policy which in 1834 might have been successful was hopeless in 1837. The distribution of the surplus money ordered by Congress was arrested because there was no surplus to distribute, and disbursements had to be made in Treasury notes, which constituted a new public debt, at the moment when the last dollar of the old debt had been paid.

In October I sailed from Fort Monroe in the ship *Caledonia Brander* with five hundred of these recruits for Tampa Bay, Florida. My classmates Hooker, French, Mackall, and Fowler accompanied me, Major Kirby of the 1st Artillery being in command. Another ship, the *Thomas Jefferson*, with five hundred other recruits sailed in company with us. We were twenty odd days on the voyage to Tampa Bay, the only incident of note on the voyage was a "conflagration" at midnight, ten days out from New York. We had a great fright, but happily no real danger, as the fire was soon extinguished. Hooker, "Fighting Joe" as he was called during the War of the Rebellion, was the hero of the night. Our evenings were passed in learning the interesting game of cards called "Brag," and our commanding officer was our amiable teacher and managed to get our spare cash. As soon as we reached Tampa Bay we each assumed command of our respective companies (mine was Company E), our superior officers being absent on sick leave, or disabled by the previous campaigns. We marched across the Peninsula to join the Expedition Colonel Pierce of the 1st Artillery was organising at St. Augustine, as a pioneer corps for General Jessup who had just been assigned to the command of the Army in Florida for the Campaign of 1837-38, which terminated in the capture of the principal band of fighting "Seminoles."

The Seminole war had commenced during the Administration of General Jackson, the Seminoles having resisted the efforts of the Government to remove them to certain reservations west of the Mississippi. General Jackson treated the outbreak as of little consequence, notwithstanding the massacre of a detachment of United States troops under the command of Major Dade in 1835. General Gaines first, and afterwards General Scott in the winter of 1836-37, had been completely baffled in their efforts to effect their removal. The Indians, who were well armed, had succeeded in inflicting great losses upon the United States troops, and always eluded them ; after offering such resistance as circumstances permitted they finally retreated to the swamps in the southern part of the Peninsula. Early in 1837 the President had intrusted the command to General Jessup, who was next in rank to Generals Gaines and Scott, and was at the time Quarter-Master-General of the Army. He had under his command General Taylor who was so distinguished in the Mexican War in 1846-47, and was President in 1848. General Taylor operated from Tampa Bay as his base, and fought the Indians early in the winter of 1837, driving them into the Everglades, an extensive swamp in the southern portion of the Peninsula extending from the Gulf to the Atlantic. General Jessup operated from North to South, driving the Indians before him, and capturing the bulk of the tribe, after defeating them in several pitched battles. The Pioneer corps of his Army was commanded by Colonel Pierce of the 1st Artillery, who marched from St. Augustine south to Rey Biscagne Bay when the campaign terminated in the spring of 1838. Colonel Pierce was a gallant, but rash commander who pushed forward, establishing posts and depots along the Atlantic Coast, keeping always in advance of the main body of General Jessup's Army, and establishing posts well provisioned and equipped for the comfort and efficiency of the advancing army. Very early in the Campaign "Osceola," one of the principal Indian chiefs, was captured and confined in Charleston harbour, where he died of grief and mortification. In the winter of 1838 we captured "Sam Jones," a little south of "Jupiter Inlet," which was not far north of "Biscagne Bay." With this capture the Campaign terminated, and some five hundred of the enemy were transported to New Orleans, and thence West of the Mississippi. Subsequently the remnant of the tribe were permitted to remain by the terms of a treaty negotiated by General Macomb, the

Commanding General of the Army, who was despatched from Washington for this special service.

It would be difficult to exaggerate the suffering of the United States troops under the command of General Pierce in this pioneer campaign from St. Augustine south to Biscagne Bay, along the Atlantic coast. I remember well the astonishment with which we witnessed the energy of our Commander on our march. We found ourselves embarrassed by an impassable swamp and thicket of scrub oaks which could only be turned by a march of several days in the interior, or by water communication through the Mosquito Inlet, a salt lake parallel to the Ocean. A reconnaissance by the engineers revealed that the water in this inlet near the shore was only knee deep, and that the bottom was hard sand. The sun was declining when this report was made, and the Colonel promptly issued an order for the command to halt for the night, and prepare three day's rations to be carried in our haversacks. At daylight he appeared at the morning roll call on horseback with his regimental staff, and led his Command into the water; for twelve mortal hours we trudged along in the water up to our knees and sometimes up to our waists, until at midnight we reached the " Haulover" which was the strip of dry land that separated the Mosquito Inlet, or " Lagoon" as it was called, from the Indian Riva Lagoon. A long inland lake of salt water supplied from the ocean by an inlet one hundred miles south of the Mosquito Inlet. We rested here a few days until we were supplied with some flat bottom boats which had been despatched to us from St. Augustine and Charleston. The Indians meanwhile who had been in ambush for us along the shores of the Mosquito Inlet, amazed at our flank movement, took to flight, and spread the most extravagant accounts of our march to the Indians south of us.

While we were waiting for our boats at the " Haulover" we erected a fort for the protection of our supplies; a small force under Captain Powell of the Navy overtook us here with a naval exploring expedition, organized at Washington, and apparently independent of the military expeditions under the direction of General Jessup, the object of which was to explore the " Everglades," the inland sea referred to between the Gulf and the Atlantic, studded with five islands, on which it was supposed many Indians were domiciled. Here I met for the first time General Joseph E. Johnston, so distinguished in the War of the Rebellion. He was then a topographical engineeer in the service of the Navy, having resigned from the Army after serving with General Scott in the Florida Campaign of 1836-37. Colonel Pierce was inclined to arrest the progress of this expedition and consolidate it with his own pioneer corps, but Captain Powell protested, and as he was acting under the special orders of the Secretary of the Navy, he was allowed to proceed. He did not go far however before he met a body of Indians near Jupiter Inlet who gave him battle and defeated him badly : but for the courage and skill of Johnston he would have been utterly destroyed. He had about one hundred sailors and a Company of the 1st Artillery under the command of my messmate, Lieutenant Fowler. He came upon the Indians in an open " Pine Barren" playing ball ; they were completely surprised, but they rallied very gallantly, and after some manœuvring were able to check Powell's advance, and very soon obliged him to retreat. Fowler was shot through the body, and Midshipman Harrison of the Navy was desperately wounded at the same time. Johnston took command of the soldiers of Fowler's Company, and covered Powell's retreat to his boats. Fowler and Harrison were carried off the field by two stalwart negroes, and Johnston held a position to cover the boats on the river, in the last of which he found refuge himself.

The whole party returned to us the next day at Jupiter's Inlet, where we were engaged in erecting another fort similar to that which we had erected at the "Haulover". It was at this fort, called "Fort Pierce," that General Jessup's Army overtook the Pioneer Corps which was consolidated with the main Army. I was ordered to reinforce Captain Powell's Expedition with Company "E" 1st Artillery, and Lieut. J.B. Magruder, who was a distinguished General in the War of the Rebellion, was assigned to the command of Lieut. Fowler's Company. Captain Powell, thus strengthened, was ordered to resume his forward movement, and to explore the Everglades. This service was performed with great energy, and in conjunction with a detachment of the main army under the command of Colonel Bankhead the Everglades were explored and the Indians found therein driven to the mainland, where they fell an easy prey to the main army, and to the number of five hundred were captured and sent to New Orleans, and thence to the Indian Reservations west of the Mississippi. This campaign in the Everglades was a novel and interesting military expedition. We had the entire command in large flat bottom boats of light draft, each boat carrying eight or ten soldiers with their arms and provisions for ten days, and ascending the rivers from the Everglades to the Atlantic, we operated in the water about knee-deep, marching by the side of the boats when the water was not too deep, and taking refuge in the boats when the depth was too great for marching. Thus we operated from island to island, day and night, guided in the night by the Indian fires on the islands — they always fled at our approach — sometimes fighting as they fled, but steadily giving way as we approached.

67

Some few captures were made, but the Everglades were completely scoured and we pursued the Indians to the mainland where subsequently they were captured. At the termination of this campaign I was ordered with my Company to Northern Georgia to take part in the campaign against the Cherokees, and remove them also to the Reservations west of the Mississippi.

This expedition into Northern Georgia was a short and decisive Campaign during the summer of 1838. I was transported from Cape Florida to Savannah in a snug little steamer called the "Osiris" with my Company "E" of the 1st Artillery, where the entire Regiment was ordered to concentrate; but this concentration was not effected there, and I proceeded in another steamer to Augusta, where eight companies of the Regiment had already preceded me. From that point we marched due North through the centre of Georgia to the North-East corner of that State, where General Eustis had the immediate command. General Scott was in chief command, and under his direction the entire Cherokee country (embracing part of Georgia, North Carolina, and Alabama) was occupied by the United States Troops. Day after day we marched through this region, following the Indians through the mountain passes and capturing them by families, for they offered no resistance. The men generally took to flight and hid themselves in the mountains, returning to their families in our camps after their capture.

This mournful campaign occupied some five or six weeks, in which time the entire tribe was captured and despatched by land to the Indian Reservations west of the Mississippi. At its close I received permission to report in person at Washington, as I had been appointed to the new Corps of Topographical Engineers just organised. I was most graciously received by the President (Van Buren), who, though separated politically, as I have elsewhere stated, from my father, took pleasure in renewing with me the friendly intercourse that had subsisted between him and my family for full twenty years. The Secretary of War (Poinsett) ordered me to return to Florida and superintend the construction of central military roads, pending which duty I was ordered to report myself in person to

General Taylor, then in command in Florida, and by him I was assigned special duty with General Floyd, of the Georgia Militia, in command of an expedition against the Seminole Indians in the "Okefinokee" Swamps.

Floyd was an eccentric but gallant soldier who marched into swamps as Pierce did into lagoons. He gave the Indians no rest. In a few weeks he captured the miserable remnant of this poor people which had taken refuge in Georgia, while the main body of the tribe had fled South to the Everglades where Jessup captured them. With this campaign the Seminole War was concluded, though in the following year General Macomb went from Washington to Florida to negotiate the Treaty by virtue of which a remnant of the tribe was permitted to remain within certain limits in the Southern part of the Peninsula.

In the summer of 1839 I was ordered North to report to Captain Canfield, United States Topographical Engineers, under whose direction a military reconnaissance was made of the Northern frontier from Fort Covington, the point of junction of the Northern Boundary of New York and Canada, to the extreme

North West. Our relations with Canada had been disturbed and unsatisfactory throughout M. Van Buren's Administration. Canada itself was almost in insurrection, and American sympathies had been active in aggravating these disturbances. Military expeditions had actually invaded Canada from New York, and Canadians under the orders of the Governor General (Head) had invaded New York and burned an American steamer, which it was alleged was in the service of Canadian rebels; to the insurrectionary movements was added an angry controversy between the Governments of Great Britain and the United States as to the North Eastern Boundary, and the search of slave ships on the African coast. Pending this controversy a reconnaissance of the Northern Frontier was made by Captain Canfield in the summers of 1839 and 1840. The party consisted of Captain Canfield, Lieut. J. E. Johnston, and myself of the Corps of Engineers. We selected sites for defensive works at all the salient and exposed points on Lakes Ontario, Erie, Michigan, and Superior, and we made up our map and report in Washington during the winters of 1839-40. These foreign complications, together with the continued financial difficulties of Mr. Van Buren's Administration, prepared the country for his defeat in November, 1840. The failure of the State Banks as Depositories of the public money was followed by the adoption of an absolute divorce of the Government and Banks, and the creation of a fiscal system under the direct control of the Secretary of the Treasury, which, with the collection of the public revenue in specie, added greatly to the commercial embarrassment which the suspension of the Banks had occasioned. Whatever might have been the merits of this policy in the abstract, it failed to give the country the relief under existing circumstances, and the Presidential canvass of 1840 was the occasion of unmeasured abuse and condemnation of Mr. Van Buren. The canvass was very exciting, and although the Banks were generally condemned, the policy of divorcing the Government from all connection with them was not generally approved. Distress was so great in the country that the people everywhere manifested a desire for change, and General Harrison, who had been nominated by all parties and factions in opposition to Mr.

Van Buren, was elected. Many distinguished and experienced statesmen in the Democratic Party seceded from it in 1840, and voted for General Harrison, among whom was Mr. Taylor himself, who was elected Vice-President on the Ticket with General Harrison. I was myself a steady Democrat, and I believed then, as I do now, that the political subserviency of the Whig Party as organised by Mr. Clay to the money power of the country was the immediate cause of all the financial distress whieh culminated in 1837, and the details of the Administration, whether wise or unwise, never influenced my judgment. I saw only on one side the ally of the privileged and protected classes, and on the other the radical defenders of the popular principle which, while it extended protection to life, liberty, and property, refused all legislation which had for its object the enrichment of the rich, and the aggrandizement of those who already possessed control of the industrial classes. The issues raised during the Administration were momentous, and Mr. Van Buren had not the moral and intellectual force to breast the storm that swept over the country, but I never for a moment faltered in my conviction that he was right in principle.

The popular fury which took possession of the country and signalized the advent of General Harrison to power was of short duration. Before the new Congress assembled in 1841 General Harrison was dead and buried, and the leading public men who had nominated and elected him, were in violent antagonism with each other as to the necessary legislation for currency and revenue. Mr. Clay abandoned this compromise adjustment, and renewed with his utmost vigor efforts to restore a protective tariff and a National Bank. In these efforts he was, happily for the country, defeated, and discredited finally in his own person by his defeat as a Presidential candidate in 1844 by Mr. Polk of Tennessee; but the struggle was bitter, reviving in its course all the issues that had rendered so memorable the Administration of General Jackson.

In the winter of 1841 I accompanied Captain Canfield to Europe under orders from the Secretary of War (Mr. Poinsett) to inspect the works in progress in Holland and Italy, for the protection and improvement of the lower Mississippi in Louisiana. We left Boston in January for Liverpool, and we proceeded thence to the Continent. Captain Canfield visited Holland and I went to Italy, where I made a close reconnaissance of the only interesting works in progress in the Tuscan Marshes, and of those already finished in the Pontine Marshes, the latter having been originally instituted by Napoleon. These researches, though interesting, were of little practical value, owing to the great cost of the works and the limited field of operations, which bore no analogy to the immense Delta of the Mississippi Valley.

In England I found almost the same circle of public men that represented the two great parties in 1831. Lord Aberdeen was still at the head of the Tory Party in the Administration of Foreign Affairs, and Lord Palmerston held the same prominent relation to the Whig Party, though with the death of King William IV. many changes had occurred in the influences of the leading statesmen of both parties. Queen Victoria, who was the reigning Sovereign, had acquired great reputation as a considerate and constitutional ruler, and her submission to the Parliamentary principle secured for her great popularity with the English people. Our own relations with Great Britain were very much embarrassed, and the difficulties with Canada were intensified by the partisanship of Lord Palmerston, who espoused the Canadian side of the controversy, and treated our Minister, Mr. Stevenson, with scant courtesy. Fortunately, at the very crisis of the controversy, there was a change of Ministry, and the moderation of Lord Aberdeen led to negotiations which resulted in the Mission of Lord Ashburton, and the settlement of all differences in the following year by the "Treaty of Washington." Lord Ashburton was a warm friend of our country, and the head of the great banking house (the Barings) which had been for many years closely connected with American interests. In Washington he found the new Administration in possession of the Government, with Mr. Webster as Secretary of State, and the angry political feeling, which resulted from the insurrectionary movement in Canada and the State of New York, exercised no longer any influence in Washington. I remained only a short time in London. In Paris I formed a delightful association with General Cass and his family, with whom I had been intimate in Washington when he and my father were colleagues in General Jackson's Cabinet. Louis Philippe, whom I had seen in the storm of Revolution in 1830, was now a Constitutional King, respected everywhere for his wisdom and moderation as a Sovereign, though struggling with the Liberal statesmen of France, and seeking to restrain the popular principles which had given force to the movement which had overthrown the Monarchy in 1830. He exercised great personal influence in the Government, and though a wise and experienced statesman, was constantly in personal conflict with the Opposition to the Administration for the time being. Constitutional Government thus became very difficult, and it was already apparent that this popular King was laying up for himself contention and difficulty with the French people.

Turkey was then, as in 1830, the bone of contention in Europe: as Ireland was the vexed and vexatious question in England. France naturally sympathized with Ireland in her struggle, and but for the influence and moderation of the King a war with England would have been inevitable. Lord Melbourne, who was the Prime Minister, was indolent and easy going, and would not interfere with his Foreign Minister, and though the Whigs were in a decided majority in Parliament they were out-booked in the Spring of 1841 for no other reason but to keep the peace with the United States and France.

I dined with Lord Palmerston in January 1841, and he spoke of my father in terms of great respect. He said that he considered Americans as " fellow-countrymen", but added that it was next to impossible to live in peace with us. I replied that perhaps the explanation of this was to be found in the fact that we were his " fellow-countrymen" and as such were fond of our own way, and too indifferent to the rights and feelings of our friends and neighbors.

Mr. Macaulay, who was at the table, laughed heartily and approvingly at my retort, and insisted upon an analysis of my genealogy which, he said, must be Scotch. I told him I was as Scotch as he could desire, but that I was also as Irish as Lord Palmerston himself.

I was obliged to give the nationality of my maternal and paternal ancestry, which embraced English, Scotch, Irish, and Welsh great grand-parents. Amid great hilarity it was conceded that I was entitled to claim all the virtues, if I must need carry all the vices of the mother country. When the cloth was removed Lord John Russell changed his seat and, taking the place by my side, told me that my father had left in England the highest possible repute as a gentleman and an accomplished statesman. A week later I dined with Lord Aberdeen who told me that he had heard of this conversation, telling me at the same time that he was greatly attached to my father, and that he hoped he would again see him as the American Minister in England. This happened in 1855. On this occasion, as he did in the controversy over the MacLeod imbroglio, Lord Aberdeen preserved the peace between Great Britain and the United States.

This occasion was the prolonged and aggravated dispute concerning the North-Western Boundary. Oregon had been jointly occupied by the United States and Great Britain for many years, and in the Presidential canvass of 1844 the Democratic Party had committed itself to the parallel of 54.40 as the true boundary line, while the British Government insisted that the Columbia River should be the Boundary between the United States and British Columbia. These two extreme propositions left ample ground for a compromise. Mr. Polk offered the parallel of 49 as a satisfactory solution of the controversy. Mr. Packenham, the British Minister, inspired by the aggressive policy of Lord Palmerston, declined this proposition without even submitting it to his Government, and Mr. Polk, exasperated by this unfriendly diplomacy, promptly withdrew his proposition and stood upon the issue of 54.40 or fight.

Under these circumstances Mr. McLane was selected by him as his Minister to England, which Mission was accepted upon condition that if he could induce the British Government to reconsider the rejection of the offer of 49 he, the President, would consult the Senate as to the propriety of accepting this compromise, thus dividing the territory which had been jointly occupied for nearly twenty years. In this Mission Mr. McLane was happily successful, Lord Aberdeen taking the responsibility of thus terminating the controversy. The Senate of the United States, on being consulted, advised such a settlement. A Treaty was accordingly negotiated in Washington and ratified by the Senate declaring the parallel of 49 to the Straits of Fuca as the North-Western Boundary Line, leaving the island of Vancouver to Great Britain, which settlement was received with great satisfaction in both countries.

I reached Paris 3oth January '41 and took lodgings at the Hotel Sinet, Faubourg St. Honoré, nearly opposite the British Embassy. As officers of the Army on duty we were presented at Court and invited to all the official balls and receptions. The American colony was not then as numerous as it has since become, but it comprised several American families of note, highly connected with French Society. Prominent among them was the family of Colonel Thorn of New York, a former purser in the United States Navy. He occupied the Palace of the King's sister in the Faubourg St. Germain and lived in great state. He had been twelve years in France, and two of his daughters had married there, as also his son, the latter to an Austrian lady of high rank. These three families occupied apartments in the Palace and contributed greatly to the almost royal retinue of the establishment. Mrs. Thorn was the daughter of a very wealthy New York merchant who provided handsomely for all his grandchildren, and left his daughter a liberal income for life, vainly imagining that his son-in-law, who had eloped with his daughter and was never recognized by him, would not possess the wealth he had sought in eloping with his wife. The old adage however that "Man proposes and God disposes" was signally illustrated in the history of their family. The eldest son, who was being educated in England, was thrown from his horse in fox-hunting and instantly killed, and the father, as his heir, came into possession of the very large fortune inherited from the grandfather. When I was in Paris in 1830 I had known the family well and received from them the kindest hospitality; they were all glad to greet me again in 1841, and hardly a day passed that I was not in the company of some of them. A month passed agreeably and rapidly in this intercourse, but early in March I left Paris for

Italy to make the reconnaissance of the "Pontine Marshes" and the "Tuscan Marshes" to which duty I was assigned by Captain Canfield, he having reserved for his own personal observation and attention the reconnaissance of the Lowlands in Holland. These duties occupied us during the months of March, April, and May. We returned to Paris in the last days of May, and then completed the maps and reports of our respective works.

In the Autumn of 1843 I resigned my Commission in the Army and was admitted to the Bar of Baltimore as an Attorney at Law. I had long desired to take this step and had been articled with General Walter, a lawyer of distinction in the District of Columbia, who directed my studies when passing my winters in Washington at an office of topographical engineers, and under his aupices I was admitted to the Bar of the District in 1840. 'The winter of 1843-44 passed most uneventfully and without clients or practice, the confinement and solitude of my office was most irksome, I gladly embraced the opportunity of mingling with political friends in the preliminary canvass that resulted in the nomination of James K. Polk for the Presidency by the Democratic Convention that assembled in Baltimore in 1844.

Mr. Calhoun was then Secretary of State and it was due principally to his influence that President Tyler devoted the best efforts of his Administration to the acquisition of Texas, a policy which was successfully consummated by his successor Mr. Polk, adding to the National Domain nearly seven hundred thousand square miles of territory, unequalled in the world for its wonderful agricultural and mineral wealth.

Mr. Calhoun was persuaded that the critical moment was at hand when the British Government would extend its authority from Honduras North along the Gulf of Mexico into Texas, menacing at once our domestic institution of slavery and our commercial prosperity throughout the world, dependant as it then was upon our cotton product. Texas had already declared its independence from Mexico, and was constituted a State, with its Western Boundary at the Rio Grande ; the Mexican Army had been defeated and driven out of Texas, and its Commander was a fugitive, but in the midst of anarchy and revolution Mexico refused to recognise the inevitable results of the war, and persisted in its intention to re-conquer the whole of the splendid Empire it had lost through the fortune of war.

The subject of domestic slavery, added to the other questions at issue, greatly excited the country, and Mr. Van Buren, who was the recognised leader of the Democratic Party, as well as Mr. Clay, who was the real chief of the old Whig Party in all the Northern as well as in all the Southern States, hesitated to give their appreciation to a policy which, however much it might promise in the extension of our National Domain, gave also to domestic slavery an extension beyond anything which had ever been anticipated. Since Texas was now organised as a slave State, and, as such, was seeking admission into the Union, Mr. Calhoun engaged in an earnest controversy with the British Minister on the question, and did not shrink from the full acknowledgement that it was necessary and proper to acquire Texas as a Slave State, and though public opinion was divided, as it always had been when the question at issue was the extension of slavery, yet the desire to extend our National Domain was very popular, and the people were willing to leave to the future the adjustment of all the controversies which might accompany it. When the Democratic Convention assembled in Baltimore to nominate a candidate for the Presidency the excitement was great, and though Mr. Van Buren was the favourite candidate, the anxiety to pledge the party to the admission of Texas prevailed, and rendered his nomination impossible. When the first Democratic Convention assembled in 1832 to re-nominate General Jackson, the division of opinion was such as to the selection of a Vice-President that the Convention adopted the rule of requiring two-thirds of the Convention to make a nomination, under the operation of which rule Colonel Richard M. Johnson, the favorite of the party, was set aside to select Mr. Van Buren, the favorite of the President. So now the two-third rule was again invoked twelve years afterwards to set aside Mr. Van Buren, the favorite of the party, to select the favorite of those who were determined to extend the National Domain from the Atlantic to the Pacific without regard to Party ties or obligations.

President Tyler, as well as Mr. Calhoun, naturally supposed that the one or the other might have been selected to carry out the policy they had originated, but that sacrifice was too great for the active and resolute partisans who constituted the Convention, and some very influential Southern Delegates desired to effect the nomination of one of their number, but the main body of the Party persisted in having for its nominee a pure and sturdy Democrat. Such a one was found in James K. Polk, of Tennessee, with whom was associated in the first instance Senator Silas Wright of New York. He declined however, and George M. Dallas of Pennsylvania was nominated. These two gentlemen represented the best elements of the Democratic Party, and though Mr. Polk was comparatively obscure as a Presidential Candidate, he had been for the best part of General Jackson's two terms the leader of the Party in the House of Representatives, especially during the interesting period of his second election and controversy with the Bank of the United States. The Party united upon the ticket, and it was elected over the Whig Ticket on which were inscribed the names of the great Whig Chieftains " Clay and Freylinghuysen."

Although the Presidential Election of 1844 involved this great issue of admitting to the Union a Slave State which was formed out of foreign territory, yet the canvass did not result in a sectional division, for several great States at the North cast their electoral votes for Mr. Polk, while Mr. Clay retained the support of the Northern as well as the Southern Whigs. Nevertheless the great acquisition of territory which followed the admission of Texas and the war with Mexico brought into action more fiercely than ever the Free and the Slave States of the Union which could not be compromised upon the principle of a geographical division, as in the case of the territory West of the Mississippi in 1820, or upon the principle of popular sovereignty, leaving to the people of the territories, as to the people of the States, plenary power over slavery within their respective borders.

The progress of these events was not rapid however, for the War with Mexico and the controversy with Great Britain as to Oregon intervened, and the whole question of territorial government was suspended until the great acquisition to our National Domain was consummated. Mr. Polk, immediately after his inauguration ordered General Taylor to take position in Texas to defend that State against the threatened invasion of Mexico, and at the same time he despatched a Minister Plenipotentiary to Mexico to negotiate for a boundary between the two countries. Contemporaneously with this negociation he despatched a Minister Plenipotentiary to England to negotiate for the boundary between the United States and Canada on the North-West which would divide Oregon, that had been jointly occupied for more than twenty years. Mr. Polk was a conservative but courageous statesman, and while he earnestly desired peace, he was resolved to defend our just territorial rights in the North as well as in the South.

The negotiations with Mexico failed, and the Army commanded by General Taylor was assailed on the soil of Texas near the Mouth of the Rio Grande, and within the District that had been constituted by law a revenue collection district of the United States. General Taylor successfully repelled the assault, defeated the Mexican Army, and pursued it into Mexican territory. Soon after the battle of Monterey I visited General Taylor, taking to him instructions from Generals Patterson and Worth to form his command, that the former might take command of an expedition then organizing for the capture of Vera Cruz and the invasion of Central Mexico. At that time I had been assigned to duty with General Patterson as a volunteer and with the rank of Major. General Taylor ordered me back to Washington with the consent of General Patterson to explain that he would detach the latter to Vera Cruz, but that the presence of General North was indispensable to the success of the operations he was conducting in Northern Mexico.

Mr. Polk cordially acquiesced in this resolution, and to General Scott was immediately assigned the chief command of the expedition to Vera Cruz and the subsequent advance on the City of Mexico, while to General Taylor was left the advance into the Northern States of Mexico. General North, notwithstanding the wishes of General Taylor, was subsequently ordered to join General Scott, and the success of the latter eclipsed even that of General Taylor at Buena Vista. Though it was the fashion of political partisans to cavil at the Administration of Mr. Polk, nothing in our history is more creditable or showed greater talent and sagacity than the conduct of the Mexican Campaign by Mr. Marcy, the Secretary of War, with whom the President maintained the most intimate personal and political relations.

My participation in the Presidential canvass of 1844 brought me into political association with the principal men of the Democratic Party in Maryland, and in the following year I was nominated by that Party to the Legislature, the State was greatly agitated on the question of State faith and credit owing to its failure to meet the interest on its public debt principally contracted for great works of internal improvement, notably the Chesapeake and Ohio Canal Railroad. Closely connected with this question was the political issue of a radical reform in the State Constitution to enlarge the representation of the people by taking population as its basis rather than territory.

Under the latter rule the State had become bankrupt, and it seemed well nigh impossible to adopt an effective system of taxation. The responsibility for this disorder did not rest upon either political party, and neither seemed capable of vigorous effort to relieve the public treasury by providing the necessary fiscal resources. The actual Governor of the State, Mr. Pratt, was a Whig, but he applied himself earnestly to this honourable work, and I gave him the most cordial support increasing all the direct and indirect taxes then in existence, and adding thereto new taxes to meet the interest on the public debt, re-establish the public credit, and completing the entire system of public improvement for which the debt bad been contracted. Many of the new taxes were regarded as oppressive, and the increase of the tax on land was considered specially burdensome. In lieu of this increase of the land tax I urgently recommended an income tax which would reach the surplus wealth and profits of the community when actually in possession, rather than to add such charges on the cultivated land as made it impossible to secure from it any profit at all. The active commercial capital of the State rallied in force against this proposed income tax, and for years the prosperity of a large agricultural section of the State was held in check by the excessive taxation to which the land was subjected.

Philip F. Thomas and Louis Lone were my associates in this Legislature, both of whom, as well as myself, were subsequently elected by the Democratic Party Governors of the State. Two years later I was elected to Congress in the midst of the Mexican War; my opponent being Mr. John P. Kennedy, a distinguished Whig and an extreme partisan who denounced the Administration of Mr. Polk as utterly unworthy the confidence of the country, alleging that it had by an unconstitutional use of the executive power brought on the war with Mexico, and that it would destroy our industrial interests by the enactment of the tariff of 1846. These two topics constituted the issues of the canvass, and covered the entire policy of the Governmement in foreign and domestic affairs.

I was now fairly launched in politics. The Presidential canvass had brought me into relations with all the leading men of the

Democratic Party. and the usual competitions for the honors and emoluments of office served to define the obligations under which men necessarily come to each other, and as my temperament impelled me to take an active interest in current affairs, I was soon able to count my own partisans within my own Party ranks, and to lead them in conflict with the opposing party. I entered warmly into the defence of Mr. Polk's Administration; I knew the President personally, and I felt grateful to him for the distinction and confidence he had shewn my father in selecting him as Minister Plenipotentiary to Great Britain for the special negotiations then pending to settle the Oregon Boundary. It was to me a source of great pride to witness his return to active political life under a Democratic Administration, and I am conscious that it stimulated my interest in its success.

In reply to Mr. Kennedy's allegation that the President had violated the Constitution by precipitating a collision between the two hostile armies, and that he had invaded Mexico, I established clearly the fact that Congress had actually admitted Texas with the Rio Grande as its Western boundary, and that it had actually legislated to establish collection districts extending to that river, and that it was the Constitutional obligation of the President to execute these laws within those boundaries, and that the actual position of the military forces under General Taylor had been selected by that General in view of purely military and sanitary considerations, the Executive taking no further responsibility in the premises than to indicate the limit of territory within which Congress had extended the laws of the United States. This statement of the case, sustained as it was by facts, was a conclusive reply to the allegations of my opponents, and met the decided and unqualified support of the people of the Congressional District by which I was elected in the Autumn of 1847.

When I took my seat in the House of Representatives in December of that year, the Speaker, Mr. Winthrop, under the influence of personal intrigue, signified his appreciation of the zeal with which I had defended the military policy of the Administration, and his respect for the commercial character and importance of my Constituency by placing me

on the Committee of the Militia. Fortunately for the Representative, the Committee
on the Militia never sat during the entire
Congress, and he was free to devote himself
to the general interests of his constituents, a
course of conduct which was rewarded in the
next Congress by his selection as Chairman
of the Committee on Commerce, the position
formerly occupied by Mr. Kennedy.

Second only to the question of the War
in this Congressional canvass was the
policy of the Government in the exercise of
the power to lay and collect taxes. Mr.
Kennedy was a zealous advocate of the principles of protection, perhaps the most zealous
of all his contemporaries. He was a disciple
of Mr. Clay; but in the advocacy of the
"American System" he was more royal than
the King, and had distinguished himself in
repudiating the Compromise Tariff Bill, under
which the duties had been gradually reduced
to a twenty per cent. horizontal rate, and
substituting for it a Bill more protective
and prohibitory than that which had brought
the country to the verge of civil war in
1832.

In opposition to this view I advocated a

revenue tariff which should be so levied that not a dollar should be collected beyond what was necessary for an economical administration of the Government, and that the lowest rate of duty which would thus supply the Treasury should be the measure thereof, leaving the question of protection aside as an incidental one, but though only an incidental one I insisted that it would ensure prosperity to all the industrial interests of the country and the cheapest possible living to all the working classes. This was the policy advocated by the President and the Secretary of the Treasury in 1832—and gave contentment to the country, until the imagination of the people became excited by the exaggeration and sophistry of those who advocated the so-called American System, which not only gave the dearest possible living to all the working classes, but which finally destroyed by domestic competition the very industrial interests it created and protected.

I was re-elected to Congress in the Autumn of 1849, and as just noted when Congress met in December, I was named Chairman of the Committee on Commerce, and reported from that Committee, and successfully carried through the House of Representatives a Bill for the improvement of rivers and harbors, founded upon the principle that the power to regulate commerce with foreign nations and among the several States involved the right and duty to improve the navigation of all navigable streams and all harbors, into and from which the commerce of the country was by law required to enter and clear, a power exclusively vested in Congress, and which it was impossible for any State to exercise except in a very limited degree, and by the special authority of Congress; a power of immense importance and, however susceptible of abuse, pregnant with benefaction to the whole country, and limited by judicial interpretation, as to the navigability of rivers, and the creation of the several Collective Districts within which the duties were to be levied upon Foreign Commerce.

These two Congresses, the 3oth. and 31st., comprised the last two years of Mr. Polk's Administration, and the two first years of General Taylor's, during which the War with Mexico was prosecuted to a successful issue, with an immense addition to our National Domain resulting from it. It was in connection with this War and the adoption of laws for the government of this domain that the Slavery Question assumed an importance unexampled in the former history of the country. Mr. Polk, upon whom fell the responsibility of executing the measures adopted by the 29th. Congress in its expiring hours for the admission of Texas, directed the War with Mexico ; and upon General Taylor, who contributed to its successful result, fell the responsibility of executing the laws which provided for the government of the territory ceded to the United States in the Treaty of Peace.

As already noted, the existing political parties were ruptured and disorganized by the discussion of the various Bills proposed for the Government of the new territories. The friends of Mr. Van Buren in New-York insisted that Slavery should be prohibited in all the territories. Mr. Seward, with four-fifths of the Northern Whigs, rallied to the support of this free soil policy, while the great bulk of the Democratic Party sustained by Mr. Clay, with a small section of the Whig Party at the North, advocated the policy of non-intervention by Congress, or a geographical division of territory by the parallel of 36.3o,

Never, perhaps, in the history of the country was the Slavery Question discussed with such vehemence, and so thoroughly, as at this period. In 1820, upon the admission of the State of Missouri, most of the issues involved were treated more or less fundamentally. Now the immense addition of nearly seven hundred million of square miles to our National Domain, half of it being already free territory, excited both sections beyond all former experience, and planted the seed of civil war which, ten years later, called millions of men to arms, and rendered necessary an immense expenditure of life and treasure from the effects of which the country has not yet recovered, and which utterly destroyed the institution of Slavery.

No intelligent and impartial observer of the debates in the 31st. Congress could fail to note that certain statesmen of the South, as well as of the North, had already determined to push the question to an extreme issue, and if they did not succeed it was due to a few leading men of the South and North supported by Mr. Fillmore, who succeeded General Taylor as President of the United States. When it was impossible to pass Free Soil

Territorial Bills, or Bills dividing the territory by a geographical line, they advocated a Compromise Bill which admitted the State of California as a Free State and provided for the government of New Mexico and Arizona, upon the principle of non-intervention by Congress with slavery.

It must be noted, however, that as this territory was acquired by treaty from Mexico, and as slavery had already been abolished in Mexico, very little confidence was entertained in the view held by many statesmen and substantially affirmed later on by the Supreme Court of the United States in the "Dred Scott" Case, that the slave-holder, emigrating to the territories, could take with him his slaves as freely as any other species of property. This Bill, therefore, was strenuously opposed by some Southern Statesmen, as it was by some Northern Statesmen, who insisted that there should be positive Congressional prohibition, or positive Congressional protection for slavery in the territories.

In 1820 the Southern Statesmen felt secure in the territory south 36.30, because they supposed the laws of Louisiana would protect the slave holder without appealing to the abstract and fundamental principle that the territory was the common property of all the States, and, therefore, open to the occupation of the people of all with the property recognized in each. So Northern Statesmen in 1820 recognizing the territory as part of Louisiana, were less concerned as to the extension of slavery therein than they were now when the territory in question was free territory. The consequence was that no union was possible between the extreme Northern and Southern Statesmen, and the Bill in question, known as the " Omnibus Bill," was passed against these extremes through the earnest efforts of Northern and Southern Statesmen, led by Mr. Clay and Mr. Cass, and supported, as I have already noted, by Mr. Fillmore, who found the passage of this "Omnibus Bill" did not satisfy either the North or the South, though its discussion in Congress seemed to intensify the sectional feeling which had already taken possession of both the great political parties in the country. Northern and Southern canvasses were held during the 30th and 31st Congresses, and Whigs and Democrats vied with each other in their caucusses in putting forward the most extreme measures. In 1848 the Free Soil Democrats, under the lead of Mr. Van Buren, had refused to support Mr. Cass for the Presidency, and his opponent, General Taylor, though supported and elected by Southern and Northern Whigs, was soon captured by the former, and had not death removed him from the field of contention he would have been deserted, as Mr. Fillmore was, by his principal Southern friends.

It would not be difficult to indicate the influential men of the North and South who constituted the extremes of this period, for although an earnest effort was made in 1852 by the old political parties to maintain their respective organizations under the lead of Generals Pierce and Scott as Candidates for the Presidency, the effort was in vain, and these extreme Statesmen continued their fierce sectional contest until 1861, when they were installed in Washington and Richmond powerless to control the storm they had let loose upon the country.

I supported the "Omnibus Bill" in the House of Representatives and in the Southern canvasses held for conference upon it and the general question; I contended that the admission of California as a Free State was the proper offset to the admission of Texas as a Slave State, and that the territories of Arizona and New Mexico could well be left to the control of the people emigrating thereto, subject to the judicial action of the Supreme Court of the United States, which could be relied on to determine the constitutional rights of the people, and that Congress could not properly, by its legislation, interfere with such rights. This view of the question was sustained in debate by Representatives and Senators from Maryland, Virginia, South Carolina, North Carolina, Georgia, and Mississippi, and in the final vote on the Bills nearly one half the Southern Representatives voted for them.

It was curious and interesting to note that though the Bills found advocates in so many Southern States the fiercest opponents were from the same States. In Mississipi, for instance, while Senator Foote supported the Bills in a series of able and most eloquent speeches, Jefferson Davis, his colleague in the Senate, opposed them with unexampled earnestness, distinguishing himself by the most extreme conclusions, seeming to believe that he could intimidate the friends of the Bills. So in Georgia, Representatives Cobb and Toombs engaged in the most earnest controversy for and against the Bills. So in Virginia, Representatives Mac Dowell and Bayley, and Senators Hunter and Mason divided the delegation of that State. In almost every State friends of concord and harmony between the States rallied to the support of the Bills as finally passed.

The Presidential Election which followed in 1852 was regarded as a popular sanction to this statement, for General Pierce, who was nominated by the Democratic Party, gave it his adhesion in principle and detail, and he was elected, though his opponent was General Scott, a most patriotic and honorable man, and more distinguished even in the Mexican War than General Taylor, who had been elected in 1848. The immediate friends, however, of General Scott were known to be inspired by Mr. Seward, and he was nominated to the exclusion of both Mr. Fillmore and Mr. Webster, who had contributed their first efforts to this adjustment of the Slavery Question.

The conflict, however, was far from its end,

for General Pierce had no sooner been inaugurated than the question of Territorial Government was again in the foreground for Kansas and Nebraska.

I was no longer in Congress, having retired at the end of the 31st Congress to fill a professional engagement in California, but I had returned to Maryland in time to take a seat in the Democratic National Convention of 1852 that nominated General Pierce, and I was by that Convention selected as the Chairman of the National Executive Committee that conducted the Presidential Canvass.

This Convention of 1852 was an interesting assembly, and in it the extreme statesmen of the Democratic Party assisted in the nomination of General Pierce; the main body of the Party supported General Cass, but the extreme Northern and Southern Delegates would not accept him. Efforts to unite the Party upon Governor Marcy of New York, or upon Mr. Buchanan of Pennsylvania, failed, though most of the Northern Delegates were willing to accept Governor Marcy, and most of the Southern Delegates were willing to accept Mr. Buchanan; finally, after many ballots and the presentation of several new names, a Delegate from North Carolina proposed General Pierce, and the Convention rallied upon him with great unanimity and enthusiasm.

I could fill pages, were I to recount all the personal intrigues and aspirations which came under my observation in this Convention, but I prefer to withold such reflexions, confining myself to a statement of the political incidents and considerations which influenced its proceedings. General Cass represented those who were responsible for the territorial legislation which embodied the principle of non-intervention with slavery by Congress. Governor Marcy represented the Free Soil Democracy of New-York, as opposed to Governor Dickenson of the same State, who was with General Cass in the Senate, and shared his responsibility ; while Mr. Buchanan was supported by the Southern Statesmen who were willing to divide the territories in Free and Slave Territory by the parallel of 36-3o.

These three sections of the Democratic Party united in the support of General Pierce. I was myself nominated by the Democratic States Convention of Maryland as one of the two electors at large for that State, and I canvassed every county in the State, and spoke in New York and Virginia, and I knew personally all the leading men from the North and the South who were engaged in the canvass. The friends of Mr. Van Buren in New-York, and Mr. Calhoun in South Carolina, joined cordially in General Pierce's support; and whatever reserves they had in mind were not presented until after his election and inauguration.

The general feeling of the Democratic Party was that the question of slavery should not be allowed to disturb the harmony of the country, but that it should be solved in the Territories by an appeal to the Supreme Court of the United States, whenever the individual right of slave-holders should be at issue therein; and it was not supposed that the Territories West of the State of Missouri, subject as they were to the legislation of 1820, would offer any embarrassment in the future.

The chagrin experienced by Mr. Seward and his anti-slavery friends, however, at the defeat of General Scott was an element too powerful to be passed without consideration, and when the 32nd. Congress assembled it was not long before the extreme elements which distracted the councils of the preceding Congress were again brought into action; aud though General Pierce manifested his desire to adhere to the issues as presented to the people in the Presidential Canvass, the demand was once more presented that, in providing Territorial Governments for Kansas and Nebraska, positive Congressional prohibition of slavery should be insisted upon, which was met naturally with the counter-demand for positive Congressional protection.

The question went round and round in the same vicious circle, the same actors, the same bad passions, the same personal aspirations, culminating in the organization of the Free Soil, or Republican Party, and the nomination of Mr. Buchanan as the Democratic Candidate for the Presidency in 1856, with General Fremont in opposition to him as the Candidate of the new Party. Mr. Buchanan was elected, but he could not secure positive congressionnal protection to slavery, or a division of the Territory by a geographical line, as he certainly desired; and the strife went on for another four years, until, in 1860, the election of Lincoln, and the utter disruption of the Democratic Party plunged the country into civil war.

Though the climax was thus protracted, the political contention was as great in the 32nd Congress over the Kansas and Nebraska Bill as it had been when the territory acquired from Mexico was in question; but nothing occurred to eclipse the wonderful display of oratory that was witnessed in the former discussion. Mr. Clay and General Cass, Mr. Foote, of Mississippi, and Mr. Douglass, were the champions of the policy of non-intervention. Mr. Calhoun, Judge Berrien, of Georgia, and Mr. Jefferson Davis, of Mississippi united upon positive Congressional protection for slavery. Colonel Benton and Mr. Seward, for positive Congressional prohibition thereof.

Mr. Benton was the personification of aggressive insolence in debate, while Mr. Seward was the most imperturable and courteous philosopher; but both held aloft the Banner of Free Soil, and stigmatized the Southern desire to extend slavery into the Territories as a cursed and wicked abuse of the Constitution. Messrs. Calhoun, Berrien, and Jefferson Davis claimed for slavery, not only the Constitutional right to extend itself to the Territory, but found in it the moral and political influence which was a guarantee of wise and conservative administration. Messrs. Clay, Cass, Douglass, and Foote rallied the good sense and patriotism of the country to the support of the Constitution, discarding all consideration of the extreme policy of either the North or the South.

The encounters between Messrs. Clay and Benton, and between the latter and Mr. Foote of Mississippi, have no parallel in our Parliamentary annals. On one occasion, after Mr. Benton had concluded a speech in which he had made some reference to Mr. Clay's political life in 1824, the latter, who was seated on the opposite side of the Senate Chamber, rose, and all aflame with passion, advanced down the aisle in the direction of Mr. Benton and, in thunder tones, asked how that Senator dared to invite attention to the past life of any man, making at the same time a gesture of seizing his cravat, was understood to refer to a scandalous anecdote in Mr. Benton's early life, when he was accused of theft, and hiding his booty in his cravat.

On another occasion, when Mr. Foote was addressing the Senate, he referred to an incident which had occurred in the Senate some days previous when a Senator, whose name he would not mention, had forbidden him (Mr. Foote) even to refer to him in debate. He said, "Mr. President, who is that Senator?" and he proceeded to describe him by reference to incidents in his public career, and finally answering his own inquiry, he said, "that Senator is commonly called the Father of the Senate, "Pater Senatus". At this instant Mr. Benton rose from his seat and rushed towards Mr. Foote, with General Dodge of Iowa clinging to him, with his arms about his neck endeavouring to stay his wrathful purposes. Meanwhile Mr. Foote took position in the centre of the Senate Chamber and drew from his pocket a revolver, which he held in his right hand, ready to shoot his aggressor. The latter, with General Dodge on his back, stopped suddenly in his advance and, pointing to Mr. Foote, cried out—"Mr. President, arrest the aggressor; arrest the assassin; he means murder". And arrested he was immediately by several Northern Democrats. His pistol was locked up, Mr. Benton retired to his seat continuing to mutter "Assassin" "Assassin". A committee was at once appointed, and the inquiry that followed served to show up all concerned as violators of parliamentary law.

Mr. Calhoun died before this territorial discussion had closed, but though he never indulged in passionnate or unparliamentary denunciation of his opponents, yet the deep conviction with which he urged the Constitutional limitations imposed upon Congress, and most notably the great principle that all powers not granted were reserved to the States or the people, created an extreme party in the South which gradually took possession of the Southern mind, and when the majority of Congress and the Executive were united in the resolution to give positive Congressional prohibition to slavery in all the Territories of the United States, the South was ready to appeal to arms, and find a remedy in Revolution or Secession.

This condition was reached when Lincoln was elected in 1860, and, unhappily for the country, the extreme Statesmen of the North took possession of his Administration and had full sway in Congress, so that the passion of the South encountered only the passion of the North, and a war between the States, though unprovided for in the Constitution, became inevitable, and men of the North and South, who proclaimed the true Constitutional doctrine of Andrew Jackson, that the laws of the United States should be executed upon individuals and not upon States, were denounced as traitors and doughfaces, and the country was delivered over to men with sectional passions ; but I will not anticipate the narrative of 1860 and 1861, until I have disposed of the preceding ten years.

Social life in Washington was not brilliant during the 30th and 31st Congresses. Neither Mr. Polk, General Taylor, or Mr. Fillmore took much interest in it. Mrs. Polk was a quiet lady, who sustained with dignity her life at the Executive Mansion, and was very much respected by those in the Presidential circle, but she took no part in general society. General Taylor's daughter, Mrs. Bliss, was a charming lady, but she had a short term of service, and her influence was not great ; and Mrs. Fillmore, who succeeded her, had even less consideration, so that during these two terms neither the President nor his Cabinet contributed much to render Washington life attractive.

Political events were, however, as I have noted, of the highest importance, and no preceding Administrations were more notable at home and abroad. The war with Mexico; the acquisition of California; and the settlement of the Oregon Boundary sufficed for the honor of the first : the Clayton-Bulwer Treaty, though it cannot be considered as redounding to the honor of the second, made it notable; while the Treaty of Washington and the settlement of the North-Eastern Boundary sufficed for the honor of the third. In domestic politics, both Mr. Polk and Mr. Fillmore were painstaking, capable, and faithful public servants. General Taylor, fortunately for his country, lived through only one year of his term; for he was, though honorable and patriotic, altogether inexperienced.

During the 3oth Congress I lived on Pennsylvania Avenue with an old colored woman (Sally Smith), an excellent cook and a true type of the Maryland and Virginia colored people. Opposite to her little box lived Mr. Walker, the Secretary of the Treasury under Mr. Polk, and not far off, on the adjoining street, lived Governor Marcy, his Secretary of War. I knew them both well, and our families were in daily communication. These two Statesmen attracted to the highest degree the admiration of the country by the ability with which they administered their respective departments. The wife of the first was the niece of Vice-President Dallas, and the great granddaughter of Benjamin Franklin. Her mother and sisters lived with her, and no family in Washington contained more grace and talent, or greater social distinction. Mr. Walker himself was as simple as a child in his temperament, and as just and kind to all about him as it was possible for human nature to be ; with these qualities he united great ability and courage, which were made apparent in his treatment of the Texas Question under Mr. Polk. I was fortunate in the possession of his immediate friendship, and when the 31st Congress adjourned in March 1851, I went to California as Counsel in the contest between the Mexican Bankers, Baron & Co., those who claimed possession of the New Almeda quicksilver mines to the valley of San José. These mines were of immense value, which was greatly increased by the development of gold and silver mining in California and Nevada; and I greatly enjoyed the excitement of remunerative professional work after five or six years of political life which was not only not remunerative, but consumed one's pecuniary resources more than it wasted my moral faculties. The Company held these mines under a Mexican grant, and the clients who claimed under the United States alleged that the Mexican grant was fraudulent ; and after years of litigation the United States, confirmed their title, and my clients, among others, were amply rewarded for their protracted and expensive contests in the courts. My own connection with the case was not of long duration, though during the year I passed in California I engaged very actively in the practice of the law. I reached California in the early summer of 1851, and proceeded at once to the Valley of San José, where the mines were situated, and there I met an old friend and companion at West Point and in the Army, Colonel Richard

P. Hammond. He was one of the most influential of the early settlers in California, and the Speaker of the House of Delegates of the California Legislature; and while he did his best to draw me into California politics, he greatly contributed to my professional success.

At his solicitation I continued up the valley into the hills, where quartz mining was pursued most actively, and where the whole community was alive with contested claims and litigations before the improvised judicial tribunals of the country. I passed months in this region, and had a new case almost every day to be submitted to the sitting magistrate and a jury, involving not only the mining laws of the neighborhood, but the laws of Mexico, and the common law of the United States and England. The trial of these cases offered an extraordinary example of the aptitude of our people for Self-Government, and their cheerful submission to the law, which was the more remarkable, as the State was as yet in its entire Governmental organization, self-made, and as such admitted into the Union.

In this mining country, I was often

obliged to pass the night in a tent, and not in camp, then a settlement where the only houses yet built were saloons and gambling houses. In such cases my bed for the night was often the table or counter, on which, during the day, figured refreshments or cards. On my return to San Francisco I was comfortably lodged in a fire-proof brick building. My professional friend and neighbor was Judge MacAlister, formerly of Georgia, and subsequently Judge of the United States Circuit Court for the Pacific Coast. Judge Ogden Hoffman, son of the Ogden Hoffman of New York and Secretary of the Navy, was at that time United States District Judge for the California District; and before long my partner and brother-in-law Philip Hamilton of New York had a large and lucrative practice. My brother Louis McLane was at that time in California, and in possession of the river steamboat trade between San Francisco and Stockton.

The controversy over the title to the New Almeda Quicksilver Mines became of small account in comparison with this general practice in the Admiralty Court, indeed, nothing was done at that time in the New Almeda case, or for some time afterwards, beyond the taking of testimony, much of which had to be taken in the City of Mexico, and I did not remain in California beyond the summer of 1852.

Among the most noted cases with which I was connected was the trial of Captain Waterman for the cruel and unusual punishment he was alleged to have inflicted upon the crew of the ship *Challenge*, and the controversy between Commodore Vanderbilt and his rivals for the possession of the steamship *Pacific* and the Nicaragua transit between the Gulf of Mexico and the Pacific Ocean.

Commodore Vanderbilt visited the Isthmus and I met him there, and after conference, I inaugurated the policy of litigation which gave him possession, not only of the steamship he desired, but of the transit itself and all the steamships engaged therein, for which, under the direction of his agent, Mr. Vanderwater, my partner and myself remained Counsel as long as we were in California.

The case of Captain Waterman caused

intense excitement in the city of San Francisco, and it would be difficult to describe
the rage manifested against him by the
sailors of that city, and those sympathising
with them. The Court-room during the
trial was guarded by special policemen, and
the Judge and the lawyers in the case had
to be escorted by the police to and from the
Court House. At that period the entire male
population of San Francisco were armed.

The community itself was beyond the
control of ordinary police discipline, and
twice, while I was there, a Vigilance Committee had formed to inflict the summary
punishment of death on those who had
violated the law. During the winter of
1851-52, when the legislature was in session,
I was urgently solicited to remain in the
State permanently, and when a United States
Senator was elected I received a compli-
mentary vote led by the Speaker of the
House and the leading member from the city
of San Francisco, Mr. Peachey.

After leaving San Francisco in the summer
of 1852, I was retained as Counsel for
Mr. MacLaughlin, who possessed th United
States grant to build the Western Pacific

Railroad, and was afterwards in Europe with Senator Latham of that State, to arrange for the sale of its bonds, which were subsequently absorbed in its sale to the Central Pacific Railroad, so that my professional life during this year became associated with future engagements which tended to make my visit to California a notable period in my life, laying the foundation for pecuniary independence, without which politics is a serious burthen and impediment to one's worldly welfare.

I returned to Baltimore by the Isthmus of Nicaragua. I had gone there by the Isthmus of Panama, and thus formed, from personal observation, the opinion that the latter, though the shortest, was the most expensive and difficult location of the two for a canal, or even a railroad; and at the same time I formed the further opinion that the United States had no interest in either, but should apply all its efforts and resources to the construction of trans-continental railroads, East and West, North and South, a policy I have ever since advocated in and out of Congress.

Immediately on my return to Baltimore

I found myself actively engaged in politics. My friends gave me a banquet to welcome my return, over which my old friend J. Parkin Scott presided, and being chosen by the Democratic State Convention as electoral candidate of the State at large, I lost no time in entering upon the canvass of the State, as the National Convention, which met at Baltimore almost contemporaneously with the State Convention, had already chosen the Democratic Candidate for the Presidency and the Vice-Presidency ; to wit : — General Pierce of New Hampshire, and William R. King of Alabama ; the latter an old friend of my father who had represented the State of Albama in the Senate of the United States since the triumphant union of the Jackson and Crawford men in 1828. General Pierce was a much younger man, but a sound Democrat and a great favorite with the New Hampshire Democracy, which was of the most orthodox faith. Notwithstanding the internal dissensions produced by the Slavery question, the Party cordially united upon this ticket, and all had the hope that its success in November would restore the fraternal bonds necessary for the preservation of the Union of the

States.

This was the key-note to the canvass. As Chairman of the Democratic Committee I conferred with General Pierce and, with his full sanction, endorsed the non-intervention policy which had prevailed in the Legislature of the 3oth. and 31st. Congresses. Mr. Seward, who was the master-spirit of the Anti-slavery agitation in American politics, continued successfully his efforts to influence the Whig Party in that direction, under the lead of General Scott, its nominee for the Presidency.

The Presidential Canvass thus conducted, notwithstanding the agitation of the previous four years, resulted in the overwhelming success of the Democratic Candidates, and to those who have witnessed the manner in which Presidential Canvasses have been conducted in recent years, it will appear almost incredible that the expenses of the National Committee in this Canvass of 1852 scarcely exceeded ten thousand dollars for printing, and other necessary election expenses.

After the storm came the calm. Soon after the result was known General Pierce sent for Governor Marcy of New-York and R. M. T. Hunter of Virginia, and tendered to the first the office of Secretary of State, and to the second that of Secretary of the Treasury; which latter declined out of deference to his State that had selected him as U. S. Senator under peculiar circumstances pending the Slavery agitation.

Governor Marcy having accepted the confidence of the President went South for the winter, after having recommended for the President's consideration James Guthrie of Kentucky as Secretary of the Treasury. These were the two wheel horses of the Administration, and throughout its term of four years they both preserved the cordial confidence of the Democratic Party, and contributed their best efforts to maintain the spirit of fraternal concord which had secured for the President the confidence and support of the people.

So much cannot be said for some of the other Departments, in which extreme sectional passion broke forth when Congress recommenced the discussion of Territorial Government for Kansas and Nebraska. At this crisis Jefferson Davis and Maclellan of Michigan seemed to find their highest privilege in representing, the one the extreme opinion of the Slave States, the other the extreme Free Soil opinion of the Northern Democracy.

Before the Slavery issue was raised in Congress on the Bills for Territorial Governments in Kansas and Nebraska, I had left the country, having been appointed Commissioner to China with the powers of a Minister Plenipotentiary accredited to Japan, Siam, Corea, and Cochin China. Commodore Perry was already in Japan engaged in the negotiations of a commercial treaty, and he was ordered to detach a vessel of war from his squadron, and place her subject to my control to facilitate my movements and to give me a home for my Legation in those countries where we had not yet established ourselves. In China alone had we diplomatic relations, and my predecessors even there had not been able to establish themselves. The English were in possession of the Island of Hong Kong, and the Governor thereof was the English Plenipotentiary to China. The Portuguese had possession of the Island of Macao, and the French and American Plenipotentiaries resided there when they had any residence in the country.

I passed through London and Paris on my way to China ; Mr. Buchanan was our

Minister in England, and John G. Masson was Minister in France. In London I found Lord Aberdeen representing that section of the Tory Party which had seceded with Sir Robert Peel in alliance with Lord Palmerston; and Lord John Russell in possession of the Government: and in France Louis Napoleon had established the Second Empire on the ruins of the Republic which had overthrown the Monarchy of July 1830; and the salient feature of the political situation was the change of relations between England and France. Louis Napoleon in establishing the Empire, had adopted the Free Trade principles in France which Sir Robert Peel had adopted in England; and Cobden was accepted as a commercial and political authority on both sides of the Channel. France was no longer in European politics in sympathy with Russia, but on the contrary was already closely allied with Great Britain in Europe and in the East. Commercial conventions and treaties admitted the manufactures and products of each country into the other at nominal rates of duty, and French Fleets and Armies were soon engaged with British Fleets and Armies in war with Russia in the Crimea, and later on, with China.

I crossed the Mediterranean in the British Steamer to Alexandria, stopping en route at Malta; and went up the Nile in a French Steamer—the English and French being then in competition for the control of Egyptian commerce and politics at Cairo. I halted for the day and rode out to the Pyramids, which I ascended under the usual guide and control of the vagabonds who left me to find my own way down at the risk of my life, until I yielded to their imposition and blackmailing.

I left Cairo some hours after my fellow-passengers by the British overland route, in a special omnibus, and crossed the Desert to the Red Sea in about twelve hours, jumping and jolting over huge boulders half buried in the sand. I embarked on one of the fine British Steamers of the P. & O. Line, and after a delightful voyage of 20 days, touching at the mouth of the Red Sea in Arabia, Bombay and Ceylon in India, and the Island of Singapore, I reached China in the early Spring of 1854, and found at Hong Kong the United States frigate *Susquehana*, under the command of Franklin Buchanan, detached from the Squadron of Commodore Perry subject to my orders.

Commodore Perry was then engaged in negotiating a Treaty of Commerce with Japan, and, as he informed me, he had concluded a Treaty with that Empire, I determined not to go there but to associate myself with his Mission, which I was authorized to do by instructions. My predecessor in China, Colonel Humphrey Marshal, had returned to the United States, and our relations with China were most unsatisfactory, as the Imperial Commission at Canton, through whom all diplomatic intercourse with China was conducted, had successfully resisted all his efforts to maintain diplomatic intercourse or enlarge the commercial privileges secured by Treaty. Sir George Bonham, then British Plenipotentiary and Governor of Hong Kong, as well as M. de Bourbalon, the French Minister, had been equally unfortunate. Yet, the Imperial Commission at Canton, without refusing to acknowledge their Treaty right, contrived nevertheless to reduce all intercourse to these commercial transactions, practically ignoring the Treaty stipulations between China and the Treaty Powers.

Soon after I reached China, Sir John Bowring succeeded Sir George Bonham as the British Plenipotentiary, and it was therefore in connection with the former that I determined to visit all the Ports open to foreign commerce, and if possible to open communications with the Imperial Government at Pekin. China, which had been absolutely withdrawn from the observation and influence of European nations, and apparently quite indifferent to all political movements at home, seemed now aroused from its sleep of ages, and was being shaken to its inmost recesses by a revolutionary disturbance. The English war which opened the Empire to the commerce of Western Nations in 1840 gave little insight to its political condition, and nothing but the actual incident of the Taping - Wang revolt was known or understood by Europeans. This chief was a vulgar villain who rallied the lowest of the population in one of the interior provinces in the South-Western part of the Empire, and announced himself as "Generalissimus" called by God to restore the Chinese Nationality, and destroy the Manchoo Tartar race.

He had received at Canton a translation of the Bible from an American Missionary, and he denominated himself the younger brother of Jesus Christ, assuming the title of Emperor under the name of " Tisnte " (Celestial Virtue). He preached in the open squares and market houses of the towns, and declared that God had revealed to him the true story of the Creation, (as stated in the Bible), and his scheme of salvation (as related in the New Testament), representing himself to be charged with the duty of exterminating and killing all who would not believe his word; and gathering together all believers over whom his elder brother Christ would come and govern in the new Empire which he was to establish. However incredible it may seem, the Chinese mind readily accepted this material idea of God and the Creation ; and, swarming as China was with secret societies, robbers and pirates, it was not difficult to overthrow the mere handful of Tartars who represented the force and authority of the Imperial Government. China had been for ages the scene of constantly recurring revolutions, and prior to the establishment of the Tartar Dynasty in

1644 A.D. not less than fifteen changes of dynasties had occurred, accompanied with bloody civil wars.

Europe knew little or nothing of China prior to the thirteenth century; the most extreme difference of opinion was entertained concerning it, some regarding the people as simple but intelligent and domestic, others as low, debased, and ignorant. The truth seems to be that the Chinese were like all other people, mixed, good and bad. Their peculiar feature was their material, rationallistic character and high civilization intellectually. The absolute nature of their Government was based upon the authority of the family, at the head of the whole being the Emperor. With the Chinese, Heaven is the origin of all Government, and their philosophy or religion is a pure fatalism. Here is found the pure idea of a King by Divine Right, whose power is absolute. It is delegated to the Ministers of State, who delegate again administrative powers to officers of Government, down to the lowest degree, which is the heads of families. The Aristocracy of the country is the literary class, and the Emperor chooses all his civil officers from this class, and every Chinaman can present himself for one of the three literary classes to which he is appointed after examination. The Town Government of China is as popular. as in New England, every man being a voter and eligible for the town council. The literary aristocracy is not hereditary. The Royal Family and that of Confucius alone possess the hereditary principle. This Absolute Government is, therefore, in one sense, a Popular Government. The entire civil and military administration of the Empire is centred in Pekin, and controlled and directed by Imperial Councils there. The Viceroys receive their instructions from the Imperial Council at Pekin, and in their turn supervise their local administrations down to the town councils and heads of families. The fundamental principle taught by Confucius, and accepted as the religion and philosophy of the Empire, is that all men, the most elevated in rank as well as the most humble and obscure, are equally bound to perform their duty and elevate one's self. Self improvement, guided by human reason which we have all received from Heaven for our regeneration and the perfection of our nature and destiny, is believed to be the first duty of a man. In my personal, as in my diplomatic intercourse with Chinese officials, I experienced a certain courtesy of manner and speech ; but their desire to avoid intercourse was always apparent, even when Treaty obligations imposed it upon them. The truth was, that all the intercourse they permitted themselves to hold with Western Nations was imposed upon them by war, and the Treaties which resulted therefrom.

Here are some extracts of my Chinese letters and despatches which will furnish an interesting account of my stay in China, and my efforts to open communication with the Viceroys and superior officers at Pekin.

Here follow Despatches :

No. 1. Hong Kong, March 20, 1854.

No. 2. Macao, April 8, 1854.

Cofl. Macao, April 9, 1854.

No. 3. U.S. Leg., on board the U.S. *St. Susquehana*, Hong Kong, April 20, 1854.

A. U.S. Leg., Canton, April 15, 1854.

No. 4. U.S. Leg., Shanghai, May 4, 1854.

I spent some months in Paris on my return from China, and was well received by the Emperor and Empress; the latter recognizing most gracioully the kindness extended by me to the French Missionaries in China, a special report having been made thereof by the French Minister, M. de Bourbolon. The Emperor himself, at this early day of his reign, manifested an unfriendly political feeling towards the United States. In his intercourse with me he complained that we had not cordially seconded his efforts to extend commercial relations with China; which he attributed to our jealousy of Great Britain, with whom he admitted he had formed a close and friendly alliance, which he said it was his wish to extend and cement. In this connection he remarked that this alliance would render France and England irresistible on the ocean. It was evidently in his mind to have me understand how important this was in view of the future commercial relations between the Eastern and Western Nations of the world. In my reply I managed to let him understand that in the United States this alliance between France and Great

Britain had already been noted, and would cool our traditional friendship for France, without extinguishing the traditional hostility of Great Britain to France. I had a conversation with the French Minister of Foreign Affairs a few days later, in which I called his attention to the Emperor's observations, and he did not hesitate to confirm the impression made upon my mind by the Emperor. At the request of our Minister to France, Mr. John Y. Mason, I wrote an informal, unofficial account of these conversations to our Secretary of State, Mr. Marcy.

I remained several months in Paris before returning to the United States, and when I met Governor Marcy he thanked me for the manner in which I replied to the Emperor, and added that he had no regret that we declined to co-operate with Great Britain and France in their hostility to China at the point of the sword. Our Minister, Mr. Mason, was then very ill, and not likely to recover; and both Mr. Marcy and Mr. Pierce urged me to continue in the Mission to China, and the latter was good enough to say that, if Mr. Mason had to retire, or if he died, I should be transferred to the French Mission. Mr. Mason, notwithstanding his illness, was a great favorite in France, and no one was better able than he to resist the unfriendly feeling of the Emperor towards our country, and I so assured the President and Governor Marcy.

I adhered to my desire to retire from the Chinese Mission, and recommended the President to appoint as my successor Dr. Parker, the actual Secretary of Legation, who had been in the Legation since the negotiation of our Treaty by Mr. Cushing opened our diplomatic intercourse with China. The President made this appointment, and certainly no living man was better qualified for the work than he, who had been for years in China as a medical missionary help since our diplomatic intercourse was opened.

When the National Convention was called to nominate a Democratic Candidate for the Presidency in 1856, I was chosen a delegate, and, as Chairman of the National Committee appointed in 1852, I called the Convention to order. The contest for the nomination was between Messrs. Pierce,

Douglas, and Buchanan, and was most interesting; for during the four years of Mr. Pierce's Administration the Slavery question had been the constant source of contention, terminating in the adoption of the principle of non-interference by Congress with slavery in the territories which, prior to that time, had been subject to the Missouri Compromise adopted when Missouri was admitted into the Union. Mr. Buchanan, who had been influential in Congress at that time, adhered to this mode of settling the question. Mr. Douglas adopted the mode of settlement proposed by General Gass in Congress, by which the power to legislate upon the question was left to the people of the Territory. Mr. Pierce had accepted this mode of settling the question, and had signed the laws for the Government of Kansas and Nebraska which embodied it. The Southern Delegates were almost equally divided upon this mode of settlement, but a large majority of Northern Delegates were in favor of the principle of non-intervention by Congress, to which finally Mr. Buchanan gave his adhesion and support, so that all three of the candidates endorsed the principle upon which the legislation in the Kansas and Nebraska Acts was founded. The Southern Delegates who were opposed to this mode of settlement, although they voted, some for one and some for another of the three candidates, made earnest efforts to induce the Convention to declare it was the duty of Congress to protect the slave-holder in his slave property; but they were not successful, and when Mr. Buchanan was nominated by the necessary vote of the two thirds of the Convention, it was with the declaration that the principle of non-intervention with slavery by Congress should be maintained ; there being a minority of the Convention opposed to such declaration composed of Northern Democrats who were of opinion that Congress ought to prohibit slavery in the Territories, and Southern Democrats, who were of opinion that Congress ought to protect the slave-holder in his slave property.

These two sections of the Democratic Party adhered to these extreme views ; the Northern section uniting with the Republican Party that extinguished the old Whig Party and nominated General Fremont in opposition to Mr. Buchanan in 1856 on the issue of Congressional prohibition of slavery in the Territories. The Southern section, though remaining in the Democratic Party to support Mr. Buchanan for the Presidency, revolted four years later, and nominated Mr. Breckinridge of Kentucky, in opposition to Mr. Douglas, the regularly nominated candidate; which division of the Democratic Party insured the election of Mr. Lincoln, and precipitated the secession of certain Southern States, resulting in civil war with all its direful consequences.

In 1859, Mr. Buchanan appointed me Minister to Mexico, under circumstances very gratifying to me, but also very embarrassing. Mexico, always greatly disturbed, was in actual revolution, the army and the church having united to overthrow the constitutional government; the latter having possession of almost all the sea ports on the Pacific and on the Gulf of Mexico, while the former were in possession of the City of Mexico and most of the interior cities and country. The President Commonfort and Chief Justice Juarez were driven from the country; the latter, in virtue of the Constitution, becoming President in the absence of the President.

In 1859, General Miramon, who was at the head of the Government, insulted Mr. Forsyth, and the latter left the country and returned to the United States. Juarez, who had been able to return to Mexico, continued the war in support of the Constitution, and occupied the city of Vera Cruz. Nearly all the other seaports, and several of the most important States of Mexico, acknowledged the Constitutional Government, and the war was confined to the country between the capital city of Mexico and Vera Cruz, Juarez being actually beseiged in the latter city.

Mr. Buchanan explained to me that he was not willing to recognize Miramon, but that he did not intend to resent the insult to our Minister by asking Congress to declare war, and that body would not take that course at that time; he proposed therefore to nominate another Minister with instructions to go to Mexico in a ship of war, and to recognize Juarez, if the Minister, in his discretion, should think he held sufficient authority in the country to be entitled to recognition, and if not, then to remain on the ship of war until the case could be reported to the President for further instructions. After conference with several Senators I accepted the Mission.

The *Brooklyn*, commanded by Captain Farragut, was assigned to the service of my Legation, and placed subject to my orders. Captain Farragut reported to me at Vera Cruz, whither I had gone in a passenger steamship the *Tennessee*, plying between Vera Cruz and New Orleans. I sent Captain Farragut on a mission to General Robles, who commanded the Mexican army operations against Vera Cruz, Miramon himself being in the city of Mexico. I had known Robles in Washington when he was there as the Mexican Minister to the United States. I authorized him to assure Robles that I would recognize Juarez as the legitimate chief magistrate of Mexico, but before doing so, I desired, if possible, to restore peace to the country which would promptly result from my recognition and its acceptance by Miramon. Farragut performed his mission promptly, and Robles assured him he would gladly bring about this result, and that he appreciated the friendly spirit in which I sought to restore friendly relations between Mexico and the United States, and thereby relieve Mexico of much suffering and possible anarchy.

Unfortunately the military and clerical party greatly distrusted the intention of the Government of the United States, and the people of Mexico were easily excited to believe that we meditated the annexation of their country, with or without their consent. It was well known that Mr. Buchanan himself desired the immediate purchase of Lower California, and the passion of our people for the acquisition of territory was well calculated to inspire their want of confidence in us. I had great difficulty in overcoming the fears and distrust of even the Constitutional Government at Vera Cruz, for Mr. Buchanan urged the purchase of Lower California, and President Juarez, with singular determination, refused to cede a foot of territory, whatever might be the consequences. I was fortunate, however, in gaining his confidence and good-will, and in bringing him to desire the friendship and commerce of the United States, which I thought would result more certainly from intimate commercial relations than from the acquisition of territory, and the mingling of our sturdy population with the Indians and Mexicans who then inhabited Lower California and the Nothern States of Mexico.

I proposed to open ways of communication between the Gulf of Mexico and the Gulf of California, and between the points of the Pacific and the Gulf of Mexico; establishing bonded warehouses at the termini thereof, with the right to protect these ways of communication and these bonded warehouses, in common with Mexico, at the same time establishing a reciprocity of trade between the two Republics. A Treaty of this nature was negotiated and received the sanction of both President Buchanan and President Juarez. It was ratified by the Senate of the United States; however the Southern advocates of actual annexation of Mexican Territory, combining with the ultra-protective and manufacturing advocates from New England, opposed it, and continued its discussion until the extreme difference entertained on the general question of slavery culminated in civil war and secession. Nevertheless the best men in the Senate were committed to the support of the Treaty. The Senate Committee of

Foreign Affairs, who recommended its ratification by that body, was composed of some notable men. Mason, of Virginia : Seward, of New York : Slidell, of Louisiana : Douglas, of Illinois, were on that Committee, and voted to report it favorably. Mr. Buchanan greatly regretted the failure of the Senate to ratify this Treaty which, he believed, would establish commercial intimacy between the two Republics, and prepare the way for the admission of all the Mexican States into our Union. I was requested to visit Washington to make explanations to the Senate Committee of Foreign Affairs, and I never returned to Mexico. My interest in the Mission terminated with the failure of the Senate to ratify this Treaty, and the imminence of the Civil War made me unwilling to leave my country and family at that time.

I saw much of Mr. Buchanan during these four months preceding the inauguration of Mr. Lincoln, and so I did of the leading men of both Parties, and I am sure that no man of either Party was more true and loyal to the Constitution of the United States than he was, but it was not a moment when either Party would accept the Constitution. On the one side was the theory of the "higher law", and on the other the spirit of revolution against the fanaticism which substituted this "higher law" for the Constitution, which was our bond of Union. Mr. Buchanan desired to adopt the policy which General Jackson adopted thirty years before, when South Carolina nullified a Law of Congress, and he asked Congress to give him the necessary provisions and processes of law which would enable him to execute the law upon individuals, and thus avoid the coercion of States.

The Congress failed to give him these powers, and allowed events to drift on until a state of war and anarchy overwhelmed society, and left the Government no alternative but to defend itself, and preserve order by force of arms. The responsibility for this civil war, which resulted in the maintenance of the Union and the modification of the Constitution of the United States, rests with the extreme men of both sections. The one determined at all hazards to persist in the purpose of abolishing slavery; the other equally resolute in its maintenance. South Carolina precipitated the issue by the action of the people in seceding from the Union and resuming her condition as an Independent Commonwealth, in which relation actual hostilities soon commenced between the State Government and that of the United States, a condition of civil war, for which no provision had been made in the Constitution of the United States. State after State, with more or less unanimity, followed the example of South Carolina and formed a Confederate Government at Montgomery, Alabama, which assumed the responsibility and direction of war with the United States. The war assumed vast proportions, and was terminated in 1865 by the surrender of the Southern Armies to those of the United States, and the action of the people of the seceded States, in resuming their political relations with the United States, and amending their several Constitutions, as well as adopting Amendments to the Constitution of the United States which abolished slavery, and created citizenship of the United States with a new order of life between people of the several States.

I was associated with Senator Latham of California in 1863 as of counsel for the grantees of the Western Pacific Road, and visited Europe and California. In Europe I found the French Empire, which I had known in its infancy, grown in splendour, and power, and wealth, until it was without a rival in Europe. The Emperor, I thought, was as hostile as ever to the Government and institutions of this country, and he was then actually engaged in the intrigue to establish an Empire in Mexico: had it not been for Lord Clarendon's influence he would have recognized the Southern Confederacy in 1864. The Duke de Persigny told me that the Duke de Morny encouraged his inclination, and that it could not have been resisted but for Lord Clarendon's assurance that the best way to get rid of the influence of the United States was to let the civil war go on until it had utterly destroyed our power, when he would be able to establish an Empire on the Gulf of Mexico. I convinced de Persigny, but not de Morny, that the Emperor did not understand the Mexican character any better than he did this country. De Morny was a great speculator, and both he and the Emperor were interested in Mexican claims and mines, and these influences prevailed in misleading them both, as well as the unfortunate Austrian Prince who was persuaded to play their desperate game in Mexico.

About this period the rage of the Radical Anti-Slavery men in the United States exceeded all bounds, to which the pro-slavery statesmen of the South responded by earnest appeals to the Southern people to continue the war until the independence of the Southern States was recognized. Jefferson Davis, the President of the Southern Confederacy, represented this sentiment, and opposed all propositions looking to peace ; while Lincoln, the President of the United States, manifested his original desire and disposition for peace on almost any terms that secured a restoration of the Union with the abolition of slavery. The opinion of the people was in harmony with Lincoln's views, and he was re-nominated in June 1864, with Andrew Johnson of Tennessee as Vice-President, by the Republican National Convention ; the extreme

Radical Republicans having already nominated, in May, John C. Fremont for President, with John C. Cochrane as Vice-President.

The Democratic National Convention nominated, in August, in opposition to these two tickets, General George B. MacLellan and George H. Pendleton, respectively for President and Vice-President ; declaring at the same time that the war was a failure, which injudicious declaration cemented the Republicans, and assured an easy triumph to their National Ticket. The Southern vote being excluded, Lincoln received 292 votes, and MacLellan 21. The Congress, which assembled in December, passed the 13th. Amendement which was substantially the same as the ordinance of 1787 which made Free Territory of Ohio and all the States of the North West, thus terminating the struggle for freedom after nearly a hundred years of political contention.

The Administration, which was inaugurated on the 4th of March with Lincoln as President, was the Administration of Johnson ; for Lincolm was assassinated April 14th and contemporaneous with this event was the collapse of the Civil War. The Southern Armies, commanded by Lee and Johnston, surrendering, the one to Grant, and the other to Sherman, who consented to their disbandment and the return of individual soldiers to their respective homes in the several States which had seceded. Actual war was followed by the hostile and revolutionary policy of the Republicans in Congress, and the amendments to the Constitution and the impeachment of Johnson who sought to stem the tide of unconstitutional legislation. Though Johnson was acquitted, Congress persisted, and in the Presidential contest in 1868 the people of the North sustained the most radical legislation, requiring all the seceded States to be re-admitted on condition of accepting this radical policy, and Grant was elected President, with Colfax as Vice-President; and in 1877, Hayes, and Wheeler, though not elected, were counted in and inaugurated with all constitutional formality!

It is impossible to comment too severely upon the incidents which accompanied this last election, and nothing in the history of the country can be found so depraved as the course of the Administration, unless it be the incidents of the election itself, and the extraordinary means to which the Republicans resorted to cover the fraud of counting in Hayes as the President of the United States. The highest men in the country were employed as missionaries to the several Southern States, whose votes, cast for Tilden, were counted for Hayes. Mr. Garfield was sent to Louisiana, and his intercourse with negro men and women which was fuliy revealed by the press and to which I will make no further reference, was a fair type of the scandalous conduct of his associates, and entitled him to the Presidential succession after Mr. Hayes had passed into the retirement from which he never emerged.

Great efforts were made by distinguished Republicans to cover the disgrace brought upon the country by Hayes' Administration. Senator Conkling of New York, a proud and brilliant statesman, sought to accomplish this by the nomination of General Grant whose prestige was greater than that of any living man in America; but the political thieves who had stolen the Presidency in 1876 secured the nomination of their principal accomplice—Garfield—who was nominated and elected in 1880 against a brilliant soldier, Hancock, who was reputed to be the bravest among the brave in support of the Union during the Civil War which, though at an end, had left the country greatly demoralized, with five millons of negro population, and as many Ḥuns, and Germans, and Irish who had been invited to participate in and share the extraordinary events of the war itself.

The Administration which followed, under the direction of Vice-President Arthur, was uneventful; the pistol of Guiteau, a wild crank, having taken away Garfield, Arthur was left to finish the term, and distinguished himself most by his amiable demeanour in society to men and women, especially the latter : but he was uninformed, and it would not be very harsh to say, ignorant in regard to all questions of political economy. The country was ready, in 1884, to dispense with any further Republican rule. It is interesting to note that it took nearly a legal lifetime to rid it of those who had metamorphosed its Constitution, depriving it of its wonderful charm which united the States, and constituted the Union, without destroying the sovereign attributes of the former.

During the Administration of Arthur I was member of Congress and had occasion to say of it then all that I have here stated, and I said it with the kindest feelings for him personally, but with great disgust for those associated with him in it. In 1882 the Democratic Party succeeded in electing Mr. Cleveland, and he did me the honor of nominating me to the Senate, as Minister to France, to which post I repaired immediately after my confirmation by the Senate, arriving there in April 1883.

I had been elected Governor of Maryland in 1881 and, during the winter of 1881-1882 interested myself greatly in those great questions which concerned the labor, and the laboring population of the world; and I had the satisfaction to see enacted by the legislature, laws, regulating the age and conditions under which women and children should be permitted to labor, and I sought earnestly to fix the time which should be the limit of labor for men, though I was not successful in establishing this latter at eight hours, which I greatly regretted; and

I have never modified my opinions nor
ceased to regret that the selfish fear of the
Capitalists of my State deterred them from
taking the initiative in this great reform,
which would have been promptly followed
by all the other States in the Union as
it was by the Congress of the United States,
in so far as the Federal Government had
any responsability in the premises.

On my arrival in France I found a great
change in the social and political condition
of the country, although I had frequently
visited Paris since my early youth. I could
recall the Dynasties of Charles X, Louis
Philippe, and Louis Napoleon, with some
observation of the Second and Third Republics. Almost all the Conservative, or more
properly speaking, Monarchical Republicans,
like Thiers and his contemporaries, had
passed away, leaving a form of Government
as parliamentary in its character as that of
1830 which he had aided to establish, and
which he directed for so many years of
its existence. The men in power when I
was presented as Minister of the United
States were, for the most part, very Liberal,
if not Radical Republicans of the Gambetta

school, notably Mr. de Freycinet, who was President of Council and Chief of the Government Republicans. Meanwhile the difficulty of maintaining a Governmental majority was daily increasing, the advancing tide of Democracy dividing the Republicans, while the Monarchical element stood ready to give the hand of fellowship to any and all who assailed the Government. Mr. Thiers had succeeded in preserving for the Royal Princes of the House of Orleans permission to remain in France, securing to them also the large fortune which they had inherited. The Comte de Paris was living in Paris, where he held a little Court, dispensing his money and smiles of favor to all comers. At the same time several important newspapers were supported by him, and the election expenses of all Monarchical candidates. who were unable to pay their own way, had a share of his bounty. With this enemy within, and fierce Democracy outside of this Royal circle, those in possession of the Government had a most uneasy and fruitless life ; for no grouping of men in the Republican Party could withstand the corrupt Parliamentary combination. One Ministry after another would disappear, and when the Parliament assembled to elect a successor to Mr. Grévy as President of the Republic it was impossible to unite the Republican Delegates upon any one of the prominent chiefs of that Party. All was left finally to hazard, and the American example of the dark horse was witnessed in the election of Mr. Carnot, in whose modest life and traditional Republicanism all other aspirants were obliged to find a master, and in none of them could they have found a more faithful servant of the Constitution and the Republic.

It is very difficult, without undue severity, to criticize the conduct of Mr. Thiers in the Convention which framed the Constitution of the Republic, for in this great crisis, as in that of 1848, his intense selfishness absorbed every impulse of his heart and mind. In the one case he sacrificed that sterling patriot, Cavaignac, to the princely despot who was elected President of the Republic; and in the other he sacrificed the essence even of Republicanism in the desire to be himself the Chief of the State, and to be surrounded by Princes and men of the Monarchy of July.

A political strife of more than thirty years testifies to his want of true political sagacity. How much longer this strife will continue, no human being can tell, but I believe that in the end the spirit of true Democracy will prevail in France, and that, without destroying her prosperity and wonderful growth in all the arts and civilization of the human family.

My grandfather, who was a Revolutionary soldier, named his son Louis, after the King of France, out of a soldier's feeling of gratitude for the King who had sent the French Army, to assist him and his comrades in establishing the independence of their country ; and I therefore could never forget that it was to a King of France, as well as to the French people, that my country owed this great debt of gratitude ; so when I criticize those who defend the Monarchical or Republican principle in France, it is without a shade of political feeling. I do not, therefore, feel embarrassed when I refer to the excess of the Democracy, or the obstinate and unpatriotic pride of the Monarchists who are capable of any combination which would weaken or destroy the

Government. I exchanged freely with them political opinions, and did my utmost to unite them in sympathy of feeling with those who governed the great Eastern Empire, through whom the Czar himself, the most absolute of Monarchs, could be let to befriend the French people, notwithstanding their Republican form of Government, as he always befriended the people of the United States, the great Sister Republic of that which is now consolidating itself in Europe.

I do not enter into personal details, out of respect for my own official character and of that of those with whom I had the privilege of official intercourse ; but, before I left the Mission I had the satisfaction to know that nearly every one of the public men who had passed in succession through the Ministry of Foreign Affairs, shared with me my opinions, and did their best to consummate such a fraternal feeling between the two Governments and the two peoples.

My Colleagues from the South and Central American Republics, especially the Minister from Mexico, Mr. Fernandez, treated me with the most affectionate regard, and when the French Exposition was held in 1889, they all united in a request that I would preside over a meeting held to express the sympathy of the American Republics for the effort France was making to elevate the arts and industries of the world. This meeting was a remarkable and vigorous expression of the American Democracy, and Mr. Tirard, the French Minister of Commerce, who was present representing the French Government, manifested the most enthusiastic delight at the fraternal spirit manifested on that occasion.

The relations between France and the United States were most friendly and sympathetic. No political questions were at issue between the two Governments during the term of my Mission. The question of admitting American pork into France had met uncompromising opposition from the French Protectionists, who were omnipotent in the French Chamber, and had not hesitated to forbid any negotiation on this subject favorable to the Hog by the adoption of formal resolutions during the term of my predecessor, Mr. Noyes. Nevertheless, correspondence between the two Governments continued, the Ministers of the United States quietly overlooking the fact that we were not less the victims of a high protective system than was France, insisted that the American Hog was a cheap and healthy article of food, and ought not to be prescribed in the interest of the French agriculturists. Several times French Ministers of Commerce, like Lockroy and Tirard, proposed to destroy the existing prohibition, substituting for it a vexatious system of inspection which appeared to our Government no more satisfactory than existing legislation.

The French system of obligatory military service was really the only question that occured during my term which offered any serious difficulty of solution; for, although the French Government would not admit to its military service any one but a French citizen, it would not recognize our naturalization of Frenchmen who had escaped from this obligation to serve in the Army by emigration to the United States during their minority ; so that practically it was very difficult to secure the release of such naturalized Frenchmen, when they returned to their homes in France, whether for permanent or temporary residence. In the main, however, the friendly feeling between the two Governments was never disturbed by this irritating question, and I must say that few cases were ever brought to my attention which deserved the intervention of our Government, as the great majority belonged to a class that sought American citizenship only to evade the laws of their own country enacted for its defence and protection.

Now and then our little Sister Republic of Liberia would seek our protection against the encroachments of French traders on the West Coast of Africa, and though our colored brethren had never sought any political consolidation with the United States, our good feeling for them served them always a good turn in their difficulties with the Frenchmen. Sooner or later they will deprive themselves even of this slight hold on us, and give themselves over to the tender mercies of both England and France, and maybe of Germany; all three of whom are contending for the trade and possession of the Dark Continent.

Social life at this time in Paris was most agreeable to the Legation and to all Americans, a large colony of whom were resident there for business or pleasure, and no small amount of time was necessary for the Minister to exchange social greetings with the French as well as with his own countrymen; these latter were generally either art students, or people of fortune, who were even more courted in Paris than at home, especially if they had the means to *doter* their marriageable daughters, who had every inclination to become Princesses, Duchesses, and Countesses; and before I left the Legation I had performed the social function of witnessing several of these alliances with the scions of the very highest French and European titles ; and I owe it to frankness to say that whenever the opportunity was afforded me, I counselled these ambitious ladies to marry at home, and time has generally proven to me that I gave them good counsel.

With the British Ambassador, Lord Lytton, and his predecessor, Lord Lyons, I had relations, not only courteous, but most friendly in a personal as well as official character, for both of them had been in the United States, the one as Minister, and the other as a member of his uncle's (Sir Henry Bulwer) Legation, and they both preserved not only a warm regard for the United States, but had a large circle of American friends, and we had much intercourse together concerning public affairs in France and in Europe; and they were both profoundly versed therein. So, with the German Ambassador, Count Munster, and with Baron de Mohrenheim, the Russian Ambassador, I cultivated the kindest and most friendly intercourse, and it would be difficult for me to estimate the value of these relations to me in the discharge of my official duties. They regarded me as more or less a partisan of the French Government, though, after all, they had to recognize that I was not only an impartial observer of it, but that I fully appreciated the wonderful community of interest which time had established between England, Germany and the United States; the Russian Ambassador recognized warmly my appreciation of the friendship which Russia had so steadily maintained for my own country, and he did not think it extraordinary that I should bear testimony to his kindness and liberality of feeling in my intercourse with the French Government.

I cannot quitt his retrospect of the period

when I directed the Legation of the United States without noting the cordial and valuable assistance I reveived from the staff of the Legation, the chief Secretary of which, Mr. Vignaud, had been for nearly a quarter of a century in its service, and was intimately familiar with the diplomatic history of Furope; and the clerk of the Legation, Mr. Augustus Biesel, had been in its service even longer, and I had the pleasure to testify to the Government on leaving the Legation, how accomplished he was in everything pertaining to his position, and unsurpassed in his industry and fidelity. Mr. Jay, the Second Secretary, accompanied me from the United States, being appointed at my solicitation, knowing him to be possessed of every qualification required in this situation. My private secretary, Mr. A. Bailly Blanchard, had some experience in the French Consulate at Tampico, and was eminently well fitted for the service to which I had invited him, as he was for any higher official position in the Legation.